UNFUDGE YOURSELF

A Parent's Guide to Happiness

LINSEY NOGUEIRA FLANNERY

ISBN: 978-1-7771756-0-3

Cover design by: Andreea Arbanas

CONTENTS

Preface	1
Introduction	3
Principle 1 – Decide to be Happy	9
Principle 2 – Avoid Negativity	23
Principle 3 – Think for Yourself	29
Principle 4 – Have a Goal	35
Principle 5 – Do One Thing at a Time	47
Principle 6 – Accept What You Can't Control	53
Principle 7 – Give Your Full Effort	67
Principle 8 – Appreciate What You Have	77
Principle 9 – Choose to Love	83
Principle 10 – Be Nice to Yourself	95

PREFACE

Being a parent can be tough. The sleep deprivation alone is enough to take down a rhino. Then your husband drinks the last of the coffee, you realize your shirt is on backwards, and it wouldn't be unusual to find yourself fashioning a baby-sized toga out of paper towel from the public restroom after your bundle of joy soils all three of the back-up onesies you packed for the day. At that point you might look around (being careful not to make eye contact with anyone else in the restroom, of course) and find that you don't feel very happy.

We *all* go through these experiences and emotions as parents. So why are some of us able to ride the wave of wet wipes and snot while others feel they are drowning beneath it? What can we do to feel good in our day-to-day so we can make the most of the all-too-fleeting days when our kids are small?

This book was not written because I have too much time on my hands. It was borne out of the fact that I noticed myself and other parents struggling when we didn't need to be. I realized there were simple things we could all do that make all the difference. Things that don't cost anything. Things that anyone and everyone can start doing today and see a difference immediately.

I don't expect you to be perfect or live all these recommendations all the time. No one is perfect. Heck, I wrote this book and I often catch myself slipping back into old habits or needing to remind myself that there is a better way to navigate those mornings that your baby calls 9-1-1 after you gave her your cell phone to get three minutes to send a work email (apologies again for that, Emergency Services). We all lead busy, sleep-deprived lives, and creating new habits takes commitment; if we keep trying to improve, however, through effort and repetition, we will see results.

Now before going any further, let me be perfectly clear about something. Parents deserve to be happy. I know we don't always believe it. Sometimes, somewhere in the back of our heads there is a little voice telling us part of being a parent is putting our own happiness on the back burner. That is not the truth. The truth is everyone deserves to be happy. Even parents. Even tired parents with throw-up on their sleeves. Being happy is not self-indulgent or something we only get to experience as children and retirees. It is also not something that needs to come at the expense of someone else's happiness. Just because we are happy doesn't mean our kids or spouses won't be. In fact, our happiness will most likely make them happier as well.

This book is a compilation of the ten ways I have found to be my happiest self. I hope it helps you find your happiest self too.

INTRODUCTION

Whether you think you can, or you think you can't, you're right.
– Henry Ford

Pregnancy is supposed to be a wondrous and magical time. You are growing a brand-new person and planning lovingly for their arrival. You get to buy tiny clothes and paint a nursery in powdery, whimsical colours. Evenings are spent cuddling on the couch with your partner and caressing your growing belly. You can eat for two.

Unfortunately, anyone who is currently pregnant or who has ever been pregnant knows that this is not the full story. Not only can it feel like a nine-month hangover, but it is a constant firestorm of people telling you horror stories of their own pregnancies and labours.

When I was pregnant for the first time I was ambushed constantly. Not being much of a sharer myself, these stories made me feel very uncomfortable, and they always seemed to happen when I had no escape – in a business meeting, in line at the grocery store, on an elevator. For months and months, it felt like all I heard about was how hard everything was going to be. Things were going to rip and tear, my husband was never going to see me the same way again, labour was going to be more painful than dental surgery and being shot all at the same time. As someone who really, *really* hates dental surgery, I was growing more and more worried about the actual birth. Just the word "tear" still makes me feel like thousands of bugs are crawling all over my skin.

But that's not all! People also tell you that things don't get better after childbirth. Once the baby arrives you will never sleep again. Your social life will dry up. No one will want to hang out with you because your life will be so incredibly dull and you will turn into one of those people who talks about their baby all. The. Time. Your career? Ha! That's over, too. You won't have the same time to dedicate to work, so all the exciting projects and promotions will go to other people. Plus, you have to take all that time off for maternity leave, and then there's mommy brain…

It was endless. There was no escaping the barrage of unwelcome information about everything from swelling to wetting to leaking. All the negativity was weighing heavily on my already significantly heavier shoulders. After a few months of these conversations I avoided all eye contact with people and started driving to work rather than risk getting cornered on a crowded subway platform. It was months before the baby would arrive and I was already convinced I had ruined my looks, my marriage, my social life, and my career. After all, these people must know what they were talking about. They had already lived through it.

Then one day the clouds unexpectedly parted. I was wrapping up a meeting with a new client who was so elegant, I spent whole meetings consciously trying not to get lost in thoughts of her perfectly pinned hair. As I was packing up my things she turned to me and said, "You know, it's not that bad." "Pardon me?" I was confused because a moment earlier we were discussing a new product launch and rapid topic shifts were not my forte while pregnant (or, admittedly, while not pregnant). "Having a baby," she said while motioning unamusedly to my belly as though it were some dirty laundry I had brought to the meeting. "Everyone makes a big deal about it, but when I had my son it wasn't that bad. You just do it and it's fine."

I nearly fell over. Not that bad? It was as though she had just told me Santa Claus was a real man living at the North Pole. This was so different from all the other things I had heard. I wanted to kiss her and her perfect hair. Thankfully, I didn't, but her comment made me realize something incredibly important. Everyone has their own experience. All the people who had been telling me their stories were telling me *their* stories. Not *my* story. *My* story could be something different. My story didn't have to be something awful. My story could be not-that-bad. It could even, maybe, possibly, be something *good.*

Don't let the noise of others' opinions drown out your own inner voice.
– Steve Jobs

In the coming weeks as my due date neared, I tried to just take things day by day. I did my best not to dwell on the negative stories I had heard and to think of the whole experience as my own. I tried to pay more attention to what I was feeling and thinking rather than what I was told I should feel or think. Everything became a little less grave and a little more calm. My shoulders felt lighter. At least metaphorically.

Two months later the baby arrived and as far as childbirth goes, it went well. No complications and a healthy baby girl at the end of it. We named her Sharkey. It was a huge relief to have the labour done with. Personally, I didn't think it was as bad as dental surgery (as I said, I really, *really* hate dental surgery).

Now my husband and I had a brand-new baby and zero parenting skills between us. So, we started with the same attitude I had adopted following my epiphany with my client. We took it day by day and payed attention to our own experience and our own thoughts. We tried to use intuition and common sense, rather than relying on what we thought we were supposed to do or feel. When I look back at that time in my life, I picture the two of us standing over her with our hands on our chins like two mechanics bent over a popped car hood trying to figure out what's wrong with the engine.

About a week after Sharkey was born, I was at a follow-up appointment with my obstetrician and she was running down her list of questions to make sure the baby and I were doing well. At the end of the list she looked me in the eye and asked how I was *really* doing in a way that I knew meant how I was doing emotionally with this whole "being a mom" thing. "Really well," I genuinely responded. "I know a lot of people have a tough go in the early days but things are going pretty well for me. I'm really lucky."

That seemed to check the final box for her and she started

collecting her things to leave. On her way out, without looking at me, she said, "It's not luck. Everyone has the same experience, – it's how you deal with it that makes the difference."

I was left alone with the baby in the exam room to marinate in that thought. Just like my client's comment a few months earlier, this idea really struck me. Now, I know it isn't quite as simple as that. Everyone has a different experience – some people have a ten-pound baby and others have a two-pound-baby. Some people have colicky babies. Some people have two babies at once. Some people have a baby without a partner. Some people have days of labour with miles of stitches and other people sneeze the baby out in the back of an Uber. The list of unique circumstances is endless. Everyone's situation is different and none are equally easy or difficult or complex or simple, but my doctor was right about the last part – it is how a person deals with their circumstances that is the key to happiness.

Everything can be taken from a man but one thing: the last of the human freedoms – to choose one's attitude in any given set of circumstances, to choose one's own way.
– Viktor Frankl

Many people think the exterior forces on our lives predict happiness, but having a big house, nice car, lots of money or a smoking hot spouse won't make a person happy. The same goes for parenting: a person could have a wonderful baby with all the help in the world and still be miserable. Conversely, a person could have all the reason in the world to be down – they could be dealing with illness or poor circumstance – but they do not give up hope and maintain an unrelenting drive forward.

I know it's hard to believe, but with a little research, I discovered my obstetrician is not the first person to reach this enlightenment. This idea is incredibly old and can be found peppered throughout history and religion. Buddha figured it out around 2,500 years ago. He is quoted as saying, "peace comes from within. Do not seek it without." Stoic philosopher Epictetus said, "authentic happiness is always independent of external conditions." Austrian psychiatrist and Holocaust survivor, Viktor Frankl said, "when we are no longer able to change a situation, we are challenged to change ourselves." The examples are endless and the message is fundamentally the same: we create our own happiness within ourselves.

The difference between the happy parent and the unhappy parent is not measured in wealth or designer diaper bags or even whether the baby is "easy" or "difficult." Happiness is not measured by circumstance. It is measured by the parent's *attitude*. You decide if the baby bottle is half full or half empty.

PRINCIPLE 1 – DECIDE TO BE HAPPY

Most folks are as happy as they make up their mind to be.
– Abraham Lincoln

The first time I clearly noticed a link between my emotional state and my daughter's mood was when I went back to work after maternity leave. The attitude that had worked so well during the final stages of pregnancy and the early stages of having a baby had been pushed aside by intense emotions and stress when I returned to work. I was finding it hard to juggle professional and personal demands. Like many working parents, I felt I wasn't giving enough at home or at the office and felt like a failure in both places. In order to give as much quality time to my daughter as I could, I had arranged an early departure time with my office, so I would be at home more during the hours my daughter was awake. At the same time, I was putting in 60-plus-hour work weeks, working both from the office and from home, which made for very, very long days.

Along with the usual challenges we all face as parents, I was also in an unusual living situation at the time. My husband, James, was embarking on a second career as a doctor and was working his way through medical school. His training was taking him all over the U.S. and his time at home was very limited. He would come home every chance he got, but as we quickly learned, medical school isn't designed for new parents. For most of the time, I was on my own taking care of the baby and working full time in an office.

I can't say this was one of my favourite times in my life. My schedule was basically this: I would get up in the early morning to get an hour or two of work done before my daughter woke up. Once she was up, I would get us both fed and ready, walk the dogs, and be on my way to her childcare. I would work until 4 pm and pick her up by 4:30 pm. We would head home, walk the dogs, have dinner and put her to bed. After that I would clean up from dinner and log back into work for another few hours before heading to bed, or more accurately, falling asleep at the keyboard. I was overtired, overextended and emotional. Oh, did I mention I was also pregnant with my second baby?

Not surprisingly, I wasn't very happy with the way things were and I fell into a very negative mindset. Coincidentally, I started to notice my daughter acting up at the precise moments I was at my worst. One of our key trigger times was when I was rushing to get to work and trying to pack Sharkey into her snowsuit to get her to childcare. It resulted in a meltdown nearly every day.

At first I didn't put two and two together. I thought she was acting up because I wasn't home with her as much as I had been when I was on maternity leave or because her routine was different or because her dad was away. I felt that crushing parental guilt of not being able to give her more of my time, energy, and attention. Then, one day when James was home, he witnessed one of our now-typical snowsuit battles and told me very plainly that she was not the problem – I was.

While I was grabbing my phone to Google divorce lawyers, I paused. I realized he could maybe, *possibly* have a point. Each day when I went to put on her snowsuit, my mind would automatically go to a bad place. It was the moment in my day that I hated. In the daily "snowsuit" moment, I felt sad to be leaving my child, felt guilty for not having enough time with her, felt exhausted for being stretched too thin, and felt dissatisfied with the circumstances at that time. But rather than seeing all those feelings for what they were, I just balled them up into anger and frustration with putting on Sharkey's snowsuit. I was angry and ready for a fight before I even got near her with the snowsuit, and naturally, Sharkey would pick up on that, reflect my own attitude back to me and would become combative as well.

I put down my phone and thought about it a little more. He was right. It was me. But oddly, rather than feeling even worse at the prospect of this being entirely my fault, I was instantly relieved. This was great news! Because if I was the problem, that meant I was in control of the problem.

At that moment, I decided I had to change my attitude. I eased up on myself, focusing on the things I could be proud of instead of repeating what I saw as my failures to myself all day. I tried to keep things in perspective and remain calm. I tried to be more aware of my individual feelings rather than just balling them all up as anger and frustration. I reminded myself that being five minutes behind schedule was not universe-ending and it didn't mean I was a bad mom. In fact, the list of things that didn't make me a bad mom was pretty big. Being a working mom didn't make me a bad mom. Needing a break didn't mean I was a bad mom. Finding my cell phone in the fridge didn't make me a bad mom. Letting my toddler walk home with a rock from the beach so she wouldn't scream and then breaking a toe because it was too heavy for her and she dropped it on my foot, didn't make me a bad mom.

I told myself there are worse things in the world than putting snow pants on a toddler (none come to me at the moment, but I am sure there are some). When my emotions got away from me and Sharkey did act up, I felt better just knowing I had to focus on myself first. I had to calm down and change the way I was thinking in order to help everyone. And usually, just thinking about this would improve my mood toward the whole situation. I was in control. I wasn't being controlled by something else. Of course, there were also times when Sharkey would act up when I was perfectly zen. But with my new revelation and zen-like attitude, I also realized I was in control of how I reacted to her meltdowns. Remaining calm, keeping things in perspective, and acting rationally seemed to help all of us.

As I continued to actively try to remain calm during challenges, to remove myself from the moment and see things for what they truly were, and to see the humour in it all, I was finding it was easier and easier to do. And Sharkey was getting easier and easier to manage.

Like most people, I had always known a positive attitude was a good thing, but I didn't realize how good a thing it can actually be. I didn't realize adopting a positive attitude could make my life easier as a parent, but that is exactly what it does. Studies show you will not only personally feel better when you adopt a positive attitude, but you will actually be better equipped to deal with your day as a happy person. A happy brain is more productive, more resilient and suffers less burnout than an unhappy brain.[1] Given all the things parents need to manage in their days, we can't afford not to have a positive attitude because every one of us can use all the productivity, resilience and burnout-prevention we can get.

Reject your sense of injury and the injury itself disappears.
– Marcus Aurelius

A person's attitude is a major predictor of happiness. Attitude has often been called "the magic word." When a person has a great attitude, they are unstoppable. Good things just seem to happen to them. They have happy and fulfilling relationships and friendships, and satisfying jobs. Life is easy for them. It might be tempting to say that they have a good attitude because everything is going so well for them but, it's likely that things are going so well for them because of their great attitude.

The way I see it, there are three aspects of a person's disposition that make up their attitude, all of which are within the person's control. You will no doubt be familiar with all three, as we have all had points in our lives when we have been better or worse at each of the aspects.

The first is how we interpret the world around us. Shawn Achor, author of *The Happiness Advantage*, argues that how we interpret our daily activities, more than the activity itself, is the primary driver of whether or not a person will be happy. Achor uses the example of two school janitors performing exactly the same tasks each day. One sees only the mess they need to clean up day after day but the other can see that they are contributing to a cleaner and healthier environment for the students. Their different mindsets around what they need to do everyday is going to dictate their personal

[1] Lyubomirsky, S., King, L.. & Diener, E. "The Benefits of Frequent Positive Affect: Does Happiness Lead to Success?" *Psychological Bulletin*, 2005, Vol. 131, No. 6, 803-855

satisfaction, job satisfaction, and likely how well they do their jobs.[2] While it is hard to tell exactly how important interpretation of the world is to our overall happiness, research suggests that only ten per cent of our happiness is determined by external circumstances.[3] This leaves 90 per cent of the control within ourselves. Ninety per cent! So how we instruct our brains to interpret our world is a huge influence over whether we will be happy or unhappy.

Take an honest look at where you stack up in this area. Are you the sort of person who dreads the day ahead or do you look forward to it? Do you see the good in people or do you think everyone is trying to screw you? Do you find you are always waiting for something better in the future or can you see the good in what's happening right now?

If you are the kind of person who is seeing a lot of negative in your environment, you can train this nasty habit out of your brain with concerted effort. Our brains are plastic and we are far more in control of our thoughts than we give ourselves credit for. Have you ever noticed how if you really want something you start seeing it everywhere? Let's say you want a cheesecake. All of a sudden you start seeing them everywhere – a new bakery pops up on route to your yoga class, your kid's new play kitchen comes complete with sliced plastic cheesecake, and, in a surprising turn of events, the paediatrician's waiting room is playing reruns of "The Golden Girls" in which none of them can sleep so they sit together in the kitchen eating cheesecake and solving their problems. The world is telling you to eat cheesecake (and reminding you what an amazing show "The Golden Girls" was!) – or maybe your brain is.

Some people say this is the reticular activating system at work – a part of your brain which acts as the gateway between conscious and subconscious thought, filtering out the billions of things that aren't relevant to you and bringing information that is relevant to you into your conscious thoughts. Looking back now, I can see that when I had kids, my brain began filtering out things like the names

---

[2] Shawn Achor, *The Happiness Advantage: The Seven Principles of Positive Psychology That Fuel Success and Performance at Work* (New York: Crown Publishing Group, 2010), 62-86

[3] Lyubomirsky, S., Sheldon, K. & Schkade, D. "Pursuing Happiness: The Architecture of Sustainable Change" *Review of General Psychology*, 2005, Vol. 9, No. 2, 111-131

of celebrities, new restaurants that were opening up, and recipes that had more than five ingredients, took longer than 20 minutes or needed more than one pot. At the same time, my brain hyper-focused on jingling dog collars that could possibly wake sleeping babies, comfortable leggings and choking hazards.

The good news is you can get your brain working on making you happier by telling it what to focus on. Put your brain to work on finding good, positive things in your day. Tell it to look for puppies and baby smiles and kindness. Those things are around all the time. We just need to tell our brains to pay attention to them.

The second aspect of attitude is how we respond to the tasks, events and happenings in our lives. Do we give up on things before we even get started because we think they are impossible? Do we grind through every day because we assume everything will be difficult? Do we dread our day because we just *know* we will run into that other new mom who is already back in pants with a proper waistband? Or do we do the opposite? Do we try new things because we enjoy a challenge and know we will persevere even in the face of failures or setbacks?

This is an incredibly important part of our attitudes because it is this part of our thinking that largely determines how successful we will be at every single task in life – everything from getting a promotion to raising a family. It determines how successful we will be with the things we undertake in our lives and even determines what we will decide to do with our lives.

Are you the kind of person who takes a risk on something you love or do you assume you can't, so you don't even try? It's such a tragedy to give up on something before you even start. As actor Jim Carrey reminds us, "you can fail at what you don't want, so you might as well take a chance on doing what you love."

Between stimulus and response, there is a space. In that space is our power to choose our response.
– Viktor Frankl

The final aspect of attitude is how we present ourselves to the world. Essentially, it is an outward projection of the previous two internal aspects of attitude – how we see our world and how we react to our world. This final aspect is what we give back to our world.

Being a cheerful and positive person is an easy way to draw good things into your life. Think about some of the factors that influence people's lives, like relationships, work, and family. As a single person looking to meet people, who would you be drawn to in a room? Would you want to strike up a conversation with the person who is laughing and smiling or would you approach the person who is sitting at the side of the group, frowning with their arms folded in front of them as though their evening sacrificing small animals had been interrupted?

What about as a potential employer? Let's say you owned a fruit stand and you were hiring people to work the check out. Two people apply for the job. One of them has past experience working a cash register but they complain for the whole interview about everything – the temperature outside, the traffic they travelled through to get to the interview, their past jobs, and that they have a weird pain in their foot. The second candidate has never had a job as a cashier but they are upbeat in the interview, smiling, willing to learn the job, and are grateful for the opportunity to work while they put themselves through school. They even made a fruit themed joke during the interview. Who are you going to hire? Personally, I am going to hire the second candidate because not only am I going to have to work with this person but my customers will be dealing with them as well and I want someone who is smiling and happy, not someone who will scare away people with their plantar fasciitis.

Now let's apply this to family. Take a look at how you behave with the people closest to you. Are you happy to see your spouse when they arrive home from being away? Do you show them that? Do you greet them at the door or do you not even drag your sorry butt off the sofa or even glance up when they arrive? Personally, I have been both of these people and I can tell you that the person who makes an effort to greet someone when they walk in will set a much different tone for whatever happens next. I'm convinced one of the main reason people get dogs is because no one greets them at the door and they just want to feel like *someone* is happy they are home.

What about your kids? Are you happy to see them in the morning when they wake up or are you grouchy and irritable? Personally, I am not a morning person and I feel absolute malice toward anything that wakes me – my alarm clock, dump trucks backing up, the sun. I also like to have at least ten minutes after I get up during which I don't have to make conversation, hear conversation, or think about conversation. Sometimes, when I am feeling really indulgent, I like to go to the bathroom on my own, without an audience. So having my kids wake me up in the morning is not a good start to the day – for me or for them. After many (many) mornings of giving my kids the evil eye from over the rim of my coffee cup, I realized something had to change. Now, I set my alarm so I'm up before my kids. This way, I can greet them like a real human being after my quiet cup of coffee. It's better for everyone: I wake up in the way I like and they get a mom when they come out of their rooms, not Danny Trejo in pajamas.

If you want to be someone who people love being around, you need to make an effort to be nice. This is especially important with those closest to us because they also tend to be the first people we drop the niceties with. Of course, I understand why that is the case. It can be challenging and tiring to put on a happy face all day long. Sometimes we don't feel we are being authentic during the day as we smile through last-minute meetings, long grocery checkouts, and crowded bus rides. So when we get home, we want to be our authentic selves. Yes! Absolutely! Be authentic and genuine. If you have had a bad day, you don't need to ignore or repress your feelings about it, but you also don't need to take your bad day out on the people you love. The people in your house are not responsible for what happened in your day. Your toddler isn't the one who moved your budget meeting without telling you, your baby didn't mess up your coffee order and your husband didn't put your phone in your back pocket so it would fall in the toilet.

It *is* possible to have a bad day and also make an effort to be kind to the people you love. Call out a greeting when you get home or when they get home. Smile at each other. Hug. Ask them how their day was and care about the answer. If you've had a crapper of a day, you don't have to pretend you didn't, but you also don't need to become a negativity grenade and explode all over the people who love you. Be honest with them. Tell them your day was terrible and see if they can help you feel better. Trust me, they will appreciate your honesty much more than if you stay quiet about it but act like a stinker to them all night.

Your home is a place where you should feel happy – always. Part of that is being nice to the people in your own home. It doesn't make sense to be unpleasant to the people we care about the most, and yet, every single one of us is guilty of it at some point. My mother-in-law has a saying: "It is the lion trainer who gets bit." She's Greek and it may lose something in the translation, but the idea is there. You bite those who are closest to you. Maybe it is because we know they will forgive us. Maybe it is just because they are there. Who knows? Either way, make a promise to yourself to change that today.

Once you have committed to a positive attitude within your own home, challenge yourself to do so in the other areas of your life. Why stop at the walls of your home? Be nice to everyone you meet. Smile. Say hello to people. Even the other new mom in the pants with a proper waistband. You will be shocked at what this small difference makes through the course of a day, week, and lifetime.

These three aspects of attitude – how we interpret the world around us, how we respond to our world, and how we present ourselves to the world – are the key to success and happiness. It doesn't matter what the situation is. A positive attitude is always an advantage and it can be applied to every and all circumstances.

So how do you get a great attitude now that you know it is the key to happiness? It's simple – not easy, but simple. You *choose* to do so. You are in control. You determine your thoughts and actions. This is not a new idea. John Milton said it perfectly hundreds of years ago in *Paradise Lost*. "The Mind is its own place, and in itself can make a heaven of hell, a hell of heaven." We make our own mental prisons – but if we make them, we can tear them down.

A great attitude is created by seeing the best in people and circumstances, reacting to life in a positive, happy way, and then turning that feeling outward as you interact with people. A person who has a great attitude is grateful for the things in their life and excited about what's coming next. When bad things happen, they keep the big picture in perspective. They shrug off negativity. They focus and concentrate on good things.

It is a simple idea but, like I said, it's not easy. Adopting a positive attitude takes some focus and effort. You have to be dedicated to it and give it your time and attention. Make a conscious effort each morning to start the day off in a positive way. Yes, even the mornings where the baby wakes you at 4 am, you step in cat barf on the staircase, and you leak breast milk all over your last clean nursing bra. I know. It's not easy. But you can do it! Try hard. Focus on the good things that happen to you during the day. My personal favourite is coffee. She never lets you down. If something drags you back to a negative way of thinking, reset and keep going. Maybe make yourself another coffee. Constantly check in with yourself throughout the day, remembering to focus on the positive. When heading off to bed, make sure your last thoughts of the day are good thoughts.

Just because you are happy it does not mean the day is perfect but that you have looked beyond its imperfections.
– Bob Marley

A positive attitude is important no matter what job or life stage you are in. It improves a person's situation 100 per cent of the time. Whenever you are feeling frustrated, angry, or sad, think about what you can do by adjusting your own perspective and attitude. Did someone cut you off in traffic? Forget it. Is your mother-in-law telling you you're balding? C'est la vie. Did your baby pull down your shirt while you were outside talking to your neighbour's teenage son? It happens to the best of us. So yes, a good attitude works 100 per cent of the time and adopting a positive attitude as a parent is perhaps the most important time in a person's life to do so. Unfortunately, at times, it can also be the most challenging.

As a parent, a person's attitude is constantly being tested and, especially in the early years, we are not always at our best. We are new to the job, sleep deprived and on call 24/7. It's hard to remember to put on your rose-tinted glasses when you are so tired you can't even remember how to work your coffee machine. The working conditions of a parent can also be tough. Your tiny coworkers can get grumpy and unreasonable, you don't get any pay or promotions, and there is no time off. But, again, even though this is one of the most challenging times in life to keep a positive outlook, this is also one of the most important times, because we are not only responsible for ourselves but for the well being of our children.

Our babies pick up on our emotions and internalize them, so what we project out to them is exactly what they will mirror back to us. Just as adults can sense when someone is stressed or unhappy, it is reasonable to assume that a baby can also sense those feelings, and that will influence the baby's mood. Alternatively, when parents are calm and happy, a baby will sense those emotions and their behaviour will reflect the feeling of contentment around them.[4]

We are all affected by the emotions of those around us. It is part of what makes us human and it doesn't matter if we are five or 105. We might understand the emotions better when we are older but they are sensed at any age. When we see others suffer, we suffer too. When we see someone smiling, we smile too. Just think of how draining it is to be around someone who is negative all the time and conversely how nice it is to be around people who are laughing and cheerful. This is the same concept advertisers are exploiting when they use footage of starving children or distressed animals to encourage us to open our wallets for charity. *If I promise to adopt 12 cats will you please take the mange-ridden dog with eyes the colour of sadness off my TV screen.* It's also why they use footage of fun-loving, happy people to sell beer and Viagra. *I want to be as happy as they are! Honey, let's get some blue pills and beer this Friday night!*

It's the same reason a presenter needs to project confidence and calm to effectively deliver a presentation to their audience. I'm sure we have all sat through a speech or presentation where the speaker was terribly nervous or where they had a completely flat affect. We feel sorry for the person who is full of nerves and we are bored to tears when the presenter seems equally bored by their own material; in both cases, the content of the presentation, no matter how brilliant, is lost on us, because nothing can get through the deafening noise of the feeling in the room.

---

[4] See Edward Tronick, "Still Face Experiment: Dr. Edward Tronick," YouTube video, 2:49, posted by "UMass Boston," November 30, 2009, https://youtu.be/apzXGEbZht0.

I've learned that people will forget what you said, people will forget what you did, but people will never forget how you made them feel.
– Maya Angelou

Think about your own home. What is the deafening noise there? Is it stress? Resentment? Fatigue? Or is it laughter, happiness, and energy?

Your household is like a company and you are the leader of that organization. As the leader, you are responsible for establishing the company culture and the tone of the organization. Everyone is looking up to you and needs your direction. If you are calm and happy and excited for the day and for the future, your kids will feel comfortable and happy being on the company payroll. If the leadership is happy, everyone is happy. The assumption is that the company is doing well, shareholders are happy, and the workers feel secure. On the other hand, if the leader of the organization looks miserable all the time, is moody and stressed, then the employees start to worry and feel insecure. I once heard someone say that the phrase to "raise morale" is misleading, because morale isn't raised from the bottom; it all starts from the top and filters down. That is exactly how it is in a household as well.

As a final point in this chapter, I want to point out that a happy brain helps us as parents but it is also important to consider the impact on our children. Our kids are constantly watching us. They mimic our words, gestures and behaviour. The attitude we display in front of them will shape how they behave toward us, how they will behave to others in the future, and even how they themselves will go on to deal with adversity throughout their lives. If there were ever a win-win situation, it would appear this is it: happy parent equals happy child.

HOMEWORK

I know. No one likes homework, but unlike calculus, this will actually be useful in your day-to-day life. This evening, before going to bed, fill out the 'To Be' list below. Include all the attributes of the person you would like to be. Do you want to be patient, kind, smart, wealthy? Write down whatever it is you want to be, no matter how far-fetched it might seem to you. My only rule is you have to frame the attributes in a nice way. Build on your positives rather than using this as a roundabout insult to your existing character. For instance, "stop being such a failure at life" is not a good one. Maybe try "being more forgiving of myself" instead.

One you are done, put the list away and read it again first thing tomorrow morning. Doing this will get your brain working on those attributes and you will start seeing opportunities to be the person you outlined as you go on with your day. Remember to continually come back to those attributes during your day. Ask yourself what the person you want to be would do in that situation.

To Be List

List the top five attributes you would like to have (e.g. being well-read):

1.
2.
3.
4.
5.

For each of the listed attributes, identify something you can do immediately to work toward becoming that person. This should be something you feel is an achievable increment from where you currently are but you should also feel free to challenge yourself (e.g. start reading a book for 15 minutes each day):

1.
2.

3.
4.
5.

For each of the listed attributes, identify one thing that could potentially derail your progress (e.g. I don't have a book I want to read):

1.
2.
3.
4.
5.

For each potential derailment, list a solution (e.g. buy a book at lunch tomorrow):

1.
2.
3.
4.
5.

PRINCIPLE 2 – AVOID NEGATIVITY

I will not let anyone walk through my mind with their dirty feet.
- Mahatma Gandhi

A lifetime before having kids, I worked in a bar as a waitress. My first day on the job was a training day, during which I was supposed to shadow one of the head servers. I quickly learned that the two of us had different interpretations of "shadowing." His version was that he would sit and drink at the bar, I would do all the work, and he would get all the tips. As he was adding up the tips I/he was getting, he started to realize they were far in excess of what he would typically make from the same bills; since there was no end to this man's charm, he began loudly complaining, saying the only reason I was making so much in tips was because I'm a girl and men don't get tipped as well as women do.[5] After a few hours of this, a table of two men who were seated within ear shot of my trainer got up to leave. They handed me a tip and said, "This is for *you*." Then they turned to him and said, "The reason she gets better tips than you isn't because she's a girl. It's because you're a dick."

The reason I'm including this story here is mostly because I like how it ends. But it also illustrates a point. Negativity will never get you the results you are seeking. Those customers were right: jerks

[5] Not true. In fact, the person who made the best tips at that bar was a man. A nice, happy, friendly man.

don't make other people happy and, in a bar, that translates into bad tips.

As writer Dale Carnegie said, "Any fool can criticize and complain – and most fools do." Parenting can drive even the most level-headed people to criticism and complaint. It's hard not to complain when you realize the poo smell you have been trying to identify for the last two days is actually coming from the front of your own housecoat, or whine a little that you almost barfed because your baby sneezed into your open mouth. Being a parent can be isolating, and we are often desperate for interaction and acknowledgement of the not-so-great parts of being parents; unfortunately, that can cause a "negativity virus" to spread through the whole parenting community.

Negativity is highly toxic. It can ruin everything from the mood of a party to a relationship. It can also make raising kids an uphill battle. And while we all experience negative feelings from time to time, some parents manage to turn almost anything into a negative. I think of these people as crab bucket parents. Not an often-used term, "crab bucket" refers to the phenomenon in which one crab in a bucket can easily escape by climbing out over the rim, but more than one crab in a bucket will keep them all trapped, as each crab trying to escape will pull the others down. As far as I can tell, it's not malicious or intentional – for crabs or humans – but unfortunately that type of negativity drags all of us down.

With all this negativity swelling amongst parents, keeping a positive outlook is harder than ever. Research shows parents report lower levels of happiness, life satisfaction, marital satisfaction, and mental wellbeing as compared to non-parents.[6] Magazines and newspapers report on all the challenges parents are faced with – financial burdens, marital stresses, career slowdowns, and so on. Anything missed by the mass media gets written about in blogs, tweeted, posted, or chatted about. No bad day is left undissected. As a result, the internet is packed with stories of nightmare kids, exploding diapers, and stalled careers. Looking strictly at what is being written about being a parent, it is not hard to understand why one recent *Marie Claire* article was about a growing movement of

---

[6] See Nattavudh Powdthavee, "Think Having Children Will Make You Happy?" *The Psychologist*, April 2009, Vol. 22, No. 4, 308-311

people who wished they never had kids at all.[7] Of course, the vast majority of the parents who tell all the nightmare stories will tell you in the same breath how much they love their kids. I was at a party where one couple were visibly giddy to be out of the house and away from their kids. "Don't get me wrong," the woman said. "I love my kids, but they are assholes." At another party, a woman told me she had figured it out in this way, "I love my kids. I just don't really *like* them."

Yes, to be a good parent, you have to sacrifice, but this is not a requirement of parenting, it is a requirement of being good at something.
– Robert Brault

As we know from the last chapter, a good attitude brings more good things and a negative attitude brings more bad things. Being submerged in that type of negativity wears away at a person. Suddenly a person who was feeling fine starts to sympathize with the others and see things in the same way. *Maybe this is too hard. Maybe I can't do it. I'm the one who is doing everything while others sit around. My wife doesn't appreciate me. My husband has no idea how much I do around here.* It can get to the point where, if you don't have horror stories to tell, you feel left out; worse, when someone does say something positive, the "crabs" jump all over them, telling them they are wrong.

If you are always dwelling on the negative aspects of something it ends up being all you see. You draw more negative things into your life, or at the very least, you keep reliving all the negativity because that is what you are replaying in your head. If you focus on the positive aspects of your day, you will start to see more and more positive. Radio personality Earl Nightingale, likened the mind to a garden. He said, "The human mind is far more fertile, far more incredible and mysterious than the land, but it works in the same

[7] Sarah Treleaven, "Inside the Growing Movement of Women Who Wish They'd Never Had Kids," *Marie Claire*, September 28, 2016, http://www.marieclaire.com/culture/a22189/i-regret-having-kids/. (accessed February 13, 2018).

way. It doesn't care what we plant… success… or failure. A concrete, worthwhile goal… or confusion, misunderstanding, fear, anxiety, and so on. But what we plant must return to us." What you grow in your mind is up to you – negativity, frustration, and resentment or gratitude, expectancy, and happiness.

Realistically, we can't avoid all negative feelings – nor should we. We know that pushing feelings down or just putting on a brave face doesn't actually solve anything, and can fester into more complicated problems. We shouldn't repress our negative feelings, but we should try to maintain proper perspective. For instance, if we are complaining about everything from the unidentified sticky substance in our diaper bag to the seemingly parent-proof clips on our newborn's car seat as though they were life-ending problems, how are we actually going to be able to focus on and tackle any true issues that might be happening?

A former boss of mine used to have a rule: if you want to complain about something, tell one person and then forget it. Don't talk about it all day long or tell your 60,000 followers. Don't let it eat at you like that. Don't give it that power. This prevents negativity viruses from spreading through an office and prevents parents from falling into a crab bucket. Tell one person – a spouse, your mom, a friend. Someone who can help you put it in perspective and hopefully laugh or sympathize about it with you. Then – and this is the important bit – forget it. Let it go. Not the pretend let it go where you bring it up again the next time you are feeling frustrated. Let it go for real. What works for me is to either find a way to laugh about it, or to think about it as something that happened and can't be changed, so there is no sense in dwelling on it. Focus on something else that makes you happy instead. It is a far better use of your energy and resources.

On the other hand, if you have something good to say – go ahead and put it on Facebook, Twitter, a blog, your forehead. The more positive things you put out there, the more it comes back to you. The internet can be wonderful if used well. The sheer volume and popularity of parenting forums, blogs, groups and handles shows how much this particular group feels the need to reach out and connect. It wasn't long ago that it was taboo to speak out about the difficulties of being a parent. The internet gave parents a place to be honest about how they were feeling, and it wasn't as PG as the media, or my beloved soap operas, made it out to be. Things can be hard and it is important that we don't feel alone in some of the day-to-day struggles. The internet can be a great place for support, but be mindful of where you get that support. Choose forums and groups with a positive overall tone, which use humour in difficult situations. Don't get sucked into the negative. Don't grow poison in your head. Grow happiness.

I laugh at those who think they can damage me. They do not know who I am, they do not know what I think, they cannot even touch the things which are really mine and with which I live.
– Epictetus

As you practise more and more to see the good in life, you will find it easier and easier to do. In fact, everything will become easier. You will be more capable and more resilient against the negative forces in your day. You will get more done and suddenly you will be one of those people good things happen to and one of those parents who seems to have it all.

PRINCIPLE 3 – THINK FOR YOURSELF

No problem can withstand the assault of sustained thinking.
– Voltaire

When I was pregnant, I knew I had to prepare for the baby's arrival. Rather than sitting down and thinking about what I might need, I Googled it. I found tons of lists online, and, for the really keen prospective parents, there were full books on what to prepare and plan. I thought I had found a pretty good list, but then my sister gave me a list that had been passed on to her from someone else, and it was even better, because it had additional notes, which meant I had to think *even less.*

"This is brilliant," I told myself. I decided my strategy for being a parent would be to text my sister all my questions. I didn't feel like reading all the books and I was wary of using Google too much because Google brings up advice from both crazy and non-crazy people and it's hard to tell who is crazy or not, unless they use ALL CAPS, which, as everyone knows, is a dead giveaway for crazy. James was in medical school at the time and warned me not to believe internet medical advice, so I figured my sister was my best bet. She had already been a mom for a couple years and she is definitely the smarter of the two of us. She had also read every book on parenting so I thought I was totally set.

My plan worked flawlessly until about six hours after having the baby. James had gone home to walk the dogs and I was on my own at the hospital with Sharkey. She had been breastfeeding fine and was sleeping in her bassinet, happy as a clam, when a nurse with a very large presence came in and told me I needed to breastfeed her.

"Yep, no problem," I said. "She's been breastfeeding and all's well. Thanks for popping in."

"When was the last time she ate?" asked the nurse.

"I dunno… like a few hours ago maybe?" I said. Shoot. Was I supposed to be writing her feeding times down somewhere? Did one of the lists say that? I wondered if the nurse would pass me my phone so I could text my sister.

"She needs to eat every four hours," said the nurse. Gosh. She sure sounded like she knew what she was talking about. Every four hours seemed pretty specific though. I couldn't imagine that was a hard four. Probably just a soft four. Like *around* every four hours.

"OK. When she wakes up, I will feed her again," I said.

"No, you have to feed her now," said the nurse. "I will show you."

This seemed odd to me. The baby didn't look hungry. She looked happy. And sleeping. She also didn't appear to have arrived wearing a Rolex so I didn't know how she would be timing her dietary needs so precisely. I'm a human person and I eat when I am hungry. Surely that must apply to other human persons as well. Even brand-new ones. Then again, who was I to question a professional? This nurse takes care of babies all day, every day, and I have only been at this for six hours.

The nurse woke up the baby and, understandably, the baby was unhappy about that and started screaming and crying. The nurse told me that was because she was hungry. I was pretty sure that was because you aren't supposed to wake up things up that are sleeping – dogs, giants, and presumably, babies. I was starting to question this nurse's expertise. So far, none of her ideas were panning out. As the baby was crying the nurse told me to go ahead and get her to eat. I tried feeding her but she was upset and not interested in eating. The nurse told me to just hold her face down on my breast until she latched on, which she demonstrated by half-smothering the baby with my breast. I didn't need to text my sister to know why this wasn't working. This was not a pleasant dining experience for anyone.

In a matter of three minutes I had gone from happily sitting beside my sleeping cherub to shoving my breast in my screaming baby's face hoping somehow she would forget I had just woken her up from her deep sleep to force-feed her. Just imagine if someone woke you up in the middle of the night and shoved your face into a plate of chicken, demanding you eat it while they held your face down. You would try to fight off your assailant and call the police. This was all because I listened to an "expert" instead of thinking for myself.

Since I'm not great with conflict, I politely asked the nurse to leave so I could "try it on my own for a bit." Dammit. I was going to need to rework my strategy. I wasn't going to be able to depend on other people to do my thinking for me. I realized I needed to think for myself and figure out what was right for me. Don't get me wrong: I still searched things online and asked people a lot of questions but then I took all that stuff that I learned and did some deliberate thinking about what felt right in my gut. What made the most sense to *me*.

If I tried something and it didn't work, I would try to figure out why. I would try to think of the baby as a person, not as a reactionary blob. I didn't wave toys in front of her face when she cried because I didn't think I would want someone to do that to me. I *never again* woke her up from sleeping because I was pretty sure she wouldn't sleep herself to the point of starvation. When she cried a little in her crib I wouldn't go running right away because I didn't think I would want someone jumping all over me every time I made a noise in my sleep. When she started eating food, I gave her mashed sweet potato first because the baby cereal didn't seem like a yummy meal to me.

These aren't the things that work for everyone; they are the things that worked for me. Life is an individual thing. Babies are individual people. What works for me may not work for you. And visa versa. That is why it's so important to think for ourselves.

A side effect of living in a culture with so much information is that no one needs to think anymore. Information is always coming at us – blaring from the radio in our cars, flashing on TVs in our elevators, tweeted at us on our phones and screaming at us from billboards. When we need to find something out, we just Google it. Once we have the information, we immediately forget it and have to Google it the next time we need it. Our phones keep all our important phone numbers and email addresses. If you are anything like me, you can't remember a single new phone number but can still remember your best friend's phone number from high school. Part of me would love to lie and say that by downloading phone number memorization to my phone, I have freed up more brain space to concentrate on other things (important things!), but we both know that is not the reality. Downloading my thinking tasks to technology has not resulted in genius-like thinking in other areas. It has simply made me less of a thinker overall.

People always say kids don't come with an instruction book, but they kind of do. Or at least we have tried really, really hard to write one. There is so much information out there on every aspect of being a parent that being a parent has become yet another area of our lives where we aren't actually thinking for ourselves anymore.

Few people think more than two or three times a year.
I've made an international reputation for myself by
thinking once or twice a week.
– George Bernard Shaw

If I didn't know better, I would say we are all trying as hard as we possibly can not to do any thinking whatsoever. We Google everything. "Why isn't my baby sleeping?" "What is colic?" "How much caffeine is too much when breastfeeding?" We also ask other people who also don't know the answers, like siblings, friends, or parents. As a last resort we might ask an expert, like a doctor, but we likely already have an answer in our head because we looked online and if we don't like what our real-life doctor tells us, we will immediately think they are a quack.

Thinking: the talking of the soul with itself.
– Plato

So many people rely on others for answers rather than giving their own instincts any credit. There is no problem with researching what what experts and other people say about hitting, crying, sleeping, or breastfeeding, but then you need to sit with your own thoughts and figure out what makes sense to you. Researching isn't thinking. You still need to *think*. You need to sit down, ideally uninterrupted, with an actual pen and paper, write down whatever the issue is, and think about the right solution for you.

Finding an uninterrupted hour in the day to think can be a challenge as a parent. If you don't have uninterrupted time, write down the problem on a piece of paper, put the paper someplace visible – taped on the wall, stuck to the fridge, on the bathroom mirror – and then try to think about it throughout the day. Keep coming back to it as often as you can. The mind is an amazing thing and will continue working on something even after we stop consciously thinking about it. We have all experienced this when struggling to remember a name or a word that suddenly comes to you three hours later. Think about all aspects of the problem and as many solutions as you possibly can. Some of the solutions you come up with will not work. That is fine. Keep thinking. You will soon start shaping a solution that does work – not necessarily the latest research on an issue, but something that will work for *you.*

We all need to get the balance right between action and reflection. With so many distractions, it is easy to forget to pause and take stock.
– Queen Elizabeth II

HOMEWORK

Choose something in your life to do some dedicated thinking about. It could be a major issue you are having but it doesn't have to be. It could be anything – what to get your mom for her birthday, how to get promoted at work, or how to be a more mindful parent. It could be coming up with twenty things that will make you a better person or thirty things you want to do before you die. It could be how to cut down on pollution or how to save the sharks. It could be how to save your marriage or how to start a new career. It doesn't matter what the topic is, but you can't text your sister or ask Google.

The point of this exercise is to get your own brain working and to give yourself the luxury of thinking about a single topic without distraction. Find a quiet place where you won't be interrupted. I like to have a pen and paper to record my thoughts and a cup of coffee never hurts.

The first time you do this, you will realize it is actually pretty hard. Especially if you haven't done any concerted thinking lately. If you get stuck, think about what other people would do in your situation. How would your mom solve the problem? What would you do if you were a superhero? What would your cat do? If you get stuck again think about the five worst things you could do or how you could make the problem worse and then come back to solutions again.

Now, realistically, your first ideas might be stinkers – a dog collar that barks, taking Nana to the rollercoaster park for her birthday. Keep at it. The best gift you can give your brain is to use it.

PRINCIPLE 4 – HAVE A GOAL

A goal is a dream with a deadline.
– Napoleon Hill

It is widely accepted that people who set goals for themselves are more successful. Yet, if you were to ask 100 people on the street what their current goal is, I bet less than five would be able to give you an answer. It seems very few people have specific goals they are working toward and I believe that this is a major source of unhappiness in our society without people even realizing it.

There are several reasons why having clear goals can make people happier. The most obvious is that it is unlikely that you will achieve something without first setting out to get it. Writing out a goal and then working towards that goal gives people purpose, direction, and focus.

I had always been a very goal-oriented person, but after having kids I found myself in a rut. Having a new baby and toddler had kept me distracted for a while but then I started to feel the effects of living each day without a real purpose or goal. I felt unsettled and dissatisfied with my days – like I wasn't doing enough of something or maybe too much of another. If I took the kids to the park, I felt good that we had quality time together, but it might have been at the expense of getting the laundry done, so I would feel like I failed. So maybe the next day I would spend the majority of my time cleaning up but ignoring the kids and then I would be torn again. Or another day I might take time for myself but I wouldn't know what to do with that time so it felt selfish and pointless. It was just time for the sake of it, rather than time spent on something purposeful.

Prior to having kids, goals had been easy for me to create and realize. Each success would naturally lead into a new goal to work toward – the next title, better office, or pay raise – but now, at home with my family, it was much harder. I felt like I was driving a car and just reacting to traffic rather than navigating to a destination. Each day left me feeling a little bit empty because I didn't know if I was achieving anything. I never felt success.

I also tricked myself into thinking I did have goals. Things like "being happy" or "being a good mom," but those goals were far too general. There is no measurement or achievable end to them, so they don't give you the same focus or sense of success that a more specific goal does. Once I realized I was missing a proper goal, I made it a priority to create one. Once I had a new goal set, I was instantly happier than I had been in a long time. Just having something to work toward gave me more energy and satisfaction, even though no other aspects of my life had changed.

The more you lose yourself in something bigger than yourself, the more energy you will have.
– Norman Vincent Peale

The second big reason why everyone needs a clear goal is this: whether you have a goal or not, time keeps going. After meeting my husband, he left his career in England to come back to Canada to be with me. He took a few courses, trying to start something new, but nothing he was doing was really bringing him the same joy that his job in England had. He started to think about going back to school for medicine but knew it would be a very long and difficult road and the amount of time it would take was a major deterrent for him. Having left an established career to start from scratch, he already had the feeling of being behind. He really wanted to do something that would ramp up quickly, but the things he could make happen quickly weren't as attractive to him as medicine. While James was visiting a friend, he commented to their dad that he wanted to pursue medicine but didn't feel he could afford the time to do it. When his friend's dad asked why, James explained that he would be 40 years old by the time he was done all the schooling and actively in his career (at the time, 40 seemed positively ancient). "But you will be 40 anyway," replied the friend's dad. "You might as well be 40 and in a career you enjoy, rather than 40 and wishing you had done things differently." I can only assume this friend's father had the goal of giving life-changing advice to people, because what he said convinced James to go ahead with medicine.

A major stumbling block to people achieving their goals, or even setting them, is that people feel they just don't have enough time. Everyone is busy these days. The plain truth is, whether you have a goal or not, the time gets filled. For those without a goal, the time usually gets filled with things that aren't as important as working toward a worthwhile goal. Setting a goal can force you to find time in your day by making efficiencies or can force you to reprioritize where you spend your time.

Many people spend a few hours a day watching TV or checking social media. In fact, the average person spends far more than a few hours a day doing those things. Recent stats from Nielsen show American adults are consuming media – watching TV, surfing the web on the computer, using an app on your tablet or phone, listening to the radio, etc. – for more than ten and a half hours a day. Over five of those hours are spent watching TV.[8] If just one of those ten and a half hours were set aside for something productive each day, that would be seven hours a week where a person could be living out their dreams instead of living vicariously through other people's lives on TV or social media.

So, what if you aren't over-consuming media, but you still feel you don't have enough time in the day to work on your own goals? Try breaking down your week to see where you are spending your time. Let's look at a standard 40-hour work week. There are 168 hours in a week. If you take away 40 for work and 8 hours a night for sleeping, there are still 72 hours available during each week. Seventy-two hours! That is a lot of time. Time that is likely getting taken up by kids, chores, errands, and family life. But do we need all 72 hours for that? Couldn't we try to set aside one hour a day to realize our dreams? That would still leave us with 65 hours in the

---

[8] "The Nielsen Total Audience Report Q1 2016," The Nielsen Company, June 27,2016, 4

week for everything else. We aren't even spending the extra hours we have in the day as quality family time, which would certainly be worthwhile. Instead, many of us are reacting to circumstances or simply going through the motions of our daily routine without giving ourselves the benefit of a destination. We fill the time with things that aren't central to what we want to do or where we want to go. By consciously focusing on our goals we will make sure we give them our time and attention and ensure they don't get put away with the kids' toys or washed down the sink with the dirty dish water.

We are kept from our goal, not by obstacles but by a clear path to a lesser goal.
– Robert Brault

The final reason why it is important to have a goal is that not having a goal puts you in a vulnerable position. If you don't have your own goal, you risk getting swept up in other people's goals. There is an old saying that goes, "If you don't follow your own thoughts, you will follow the thoughts of the fellow who followed his." While it is a bit of an awkward saying, I believe it is accurate. After leaving England and before going to medical school, James told me that he felt like he was just tumbling along beside me, going in the direction I wanted to go in life, because he didn't have a firm direction of his own. It wasn't until he committed to the goal of medical school that he finally felt he had some direction. This can happen with a boyfriend or girlfriend, a spouse, a close friend, or even just the general crowd of people you hang out with. A goal is a powerful thing. It is important to have your own so you aren't at the mercy of someone else's.

Before heading back to work following my first mat leave, I set a goal to spend dedicated time with Sharkey each day. Time that was just for us without the distractions of the phone or work emails. I knew I was going back into an environment that expanded to fill all spaces, so to speak. Any time I would give to work, it would happily take. It was an environment that was fast-paced, client service-oriented and exciting, so it was easy for a person's personal life to get railroaded.

In the past, I had tolerated the long hours and demands on my time – sometimes even relishing the busyness and distractions of work – but things were different for me now, and I wanted to ensure I could meet the demands of work without sacrificing all my family time. With my goal in place, I felt a little more comfortable with my return to work. I was confident that strict compartmentalization would enable me to successfully meet both work and family demands, making the most of my time at the office and my time with my family.

In order to maximize the time I had with Sharkey, I met with my boss before returning to arrange the flexible schedule I mentioned earlier: I would leave the office a bit early to pick her up from childcare and then make up that time from home after she went to bed. My boss was amenable to this schedule, provided there were no complaints from colleagues or clients.

The first few months back at work were an adjustment. It was hard to be away from Sharkey during the day but I looked forward to that dedicated time with her each afternoon. There were a couple of occasions in our set family time when I needed to take an "emergency" phone call or respond to an email, but for the most part, I kept that time protected and I would always be back online after she went to bed to finish out my workday and respond to anything that had come in while I was "dark."

Then one day my boss called me into his office because one of my colleagues had shown some concern about my lack of availability in the late afternoon and early evening. To say I was surprised was an understatement. Despite my protected "family window" I was still a top performer at the office, and because Sharkey was going to bed so early, my "dark time" was really only a couple of hours. However, it wasn't the unreasonableness of the complaint that was the hardest part, it was that I felt like a failure. I had been trying really hard to be just as good at my job as I had been before having kids and receiving this complaint showed me that I simply could not give work everything I had given it in the past.

Then my boss asked if I could switch back to a regular work day and make sure I was available after work hours. As someone who was not used to getting negative feedback and who usually says yes to everything, my immediate gut reaction was to agree and go back to a typical work day. Then I remembered the goal I had set for myself before returning to work: to have dedicated time with

Sharkey each day. Time just for her where I wasn't speaking on the phone through dinner or texting during her bath time. I wanted to sit with her each night to read a story and I didn't want a buzzing iPhone beside us on the nightstand, interrupting the story and my presence in the moment.

I told my boss I was still dedicated to my job and to giving one hundred and ten percent but that block of time I dedicated to my family was extremely important to me and I simply couldn't give it up. To my boss' credit, he said he understood and that the person who complained would have to reach me outside of my family time.

Having my goal firmly in my mind gave me the confidence to push back on my boss' request. Without a goal, I would likely have been swayed by my colleagues' pressure to be more available, thus giving up a lot more than my colleague could have gained by having me instantly available to her.

There are always going to be pressures on us and demands on our time. If you don't have a clear goal, unimportant things start to creep in. It happens slowly, when we are tired or distracted. We give a little here and a little there and all of a sudden we are very far from the place we want to be. By having a clear goal, you steel yourself against this erosion of time. All of a sudden you have a purpose and a reason to keep a little time for yourself. You have a reason to say no. You have a focused idea of where you are headed and that is the biggest step toward making the dreams in your head into reality.

All that we are is the result of what we have thought.
– Buddha

The next step now is an obvious one. You need to set a goal. This is simple – not easy, but simple. It requires dedicated time and attention, which will be the first and possibly the biggest obstacle for many of us.

How are you going to find uninterrupted time? As discussed earlier, this might seem impossible and yes, it may take a few attempts. The best way for me to get uninterrupted time is to get up before the others in my house are awake. For those who are already sleep-deprived, this may not seem like, or be, the best way. What about trying to find time during a nap or after the kids go to bed? For those with young babies, perhaps going for a walk with the stroller would give you time to think. Take a pen and paper so you can write things down as they come to you. If there is someone who can watch the kids for an hour, you can pop over to a coffee shop or library. A time may even come to you when you suddenly have a moment to yourself; be prepared with pen and paper, so you can use that time productively.

If you truly can't get uninterrupted time, try to actively think about what your goal will be throughout the day. Put a note for yourself on the bathroom mirror, on the fridge, in your car, on your phone, etc. and then keep bringing your thoughts back to your goal as you go about your regular activities. Keep your paper and pen handy so you can write things down. It isn't as good as uninterrupted time but it is much better to start something than to do nothing. The important thing is not to give up. It might be difficult and your first few attempts might fail. Keep focused. This is important and your goals deserve the effort.

So now, let's assume you have found time to yourself. The next challenge is setting the actual goal. A good goal should be a few things:

1. Challenging
2. Specific
3. Carefully considered

Your goal needs to be challenging because if it is something you are already doing or an easy addition, it isn't something that will give you a true sense of satisfaction. Try to stretch yourself a little. Get outside your comfort zone. Think of your full potential and look at all the things you could be doing. Our minds tend to want to keep us within certain limitations and we need to train our brains to think beyond the normal boundaries we set for ourselves. The bigger the goal you set, the bigger your achievements and satisfaction will be.

The greater danger for most of us lies in not setting our aim too high and falling short; but in setting our aim too low, and achieving our mark.
– Michelangelo

A goal also needs to be specific. As mentioned previously, goals like "being happy" or "being a good parent" are too general. Maybe you want to be more educated. Decide how you will do that. Will you read a book each month or will you take courses online or at a local college? Maybe your goal will be to complete a nutrition course online and to be signed up to the first level before the end of the month. Great. That is specific. Maybe you want to make more money. Set a figure you would like to make and a date by which you will achieve it to make it tangible. You don't need to know how you will do it; you just need to know what you will do. Maybe you want to start a blog, write a book, run a marathon, start your own business, or volunteer. Your goal can be anything you like. It just needs to be detailed enough so you know exactly where you are going and so you will know exactly when you get there.

Next, write down the first step you will take toward your goal. You don't have to know exactly how you will get to your goal – in fact, you likely won't know – but if you write down the very first thing you need to do, you will have something to start on immediately. If you are training for a marathon, your first step might be to go for a one-mile run. If you want to become a famous actor, your first step might be to sign up for an acting workshop in your area. If you want to healthy dinners every night, you might make a meal plan for the week. Writing down your very first step sets you up for success by determining exactly what you need to do to start on your journey; then, once you've started, you might as well keep going.

Don't do nothing because you can't do everything.
– Colleeen Patrick-Goudreau

Before leaving this chapter, I want to say that having kids isn't a reason to give up on your dreams. So often people use kids as an excuse to stop doing the things they love, which is a tragedy for two reasons. First, it isn't necessary. Unless what you love is hard-core drugs and robbing old ladies, you can still pursue your interests as a parent. It might take longer than if you had 100 per cent of your time to focus on it, but sharing your focus with your kids doesn't mean you can't still spend time on the things you enjoy.

Giving up your dreams for your children might also lead to unfairly blaming or resenting them when you look back on your life and haven't achieved what you wanted to. Kids are an easy excuse to not take risks or pursue things that might be challenging, but the reality is no other person is the barrier to whatever you want to do. Even very small, demanding people. The only obstacles are in your mind, and if you want something badly enough, you will get around anything that becomes a challenge. You are the only person who can decide to do or not do something. It has nothing to do with kids.

If you want your kids to be happy, you need to show them what happy looks like, and the best way to do that is to be happy yourself. Anything you want your kids to do, you need to do yourself. If you want them to follow their dreams, treat animals kindly, clean up after themselves, exercise, appreciate the arts, or anything else, you need to show them by example.

Our kids need our time and attention but they don't need 24 hours of our day. They need us to be genuinely engaged when we are with them. They need to feel loved and supported always, but not at the cost of our own interests and dreams. Those dreams could be anything from reading up on a topic you love to competing in the Olympics, and while it might be harder than it was before kids to find the time or motivation, if you are truly committed to doing them, you will make the time and find the motivation.

The world is filled with regular people doing amazing things. Many of those regular people are also parents. Ask yourself, why not you? Why can't you be a pilot, start a dog walking business, or go to circus school? You owe it to yourself, to your kids, and to the world to live up to your potential.

You will benefit from doing things you love and your kids will benefit too. The joy you get from doing what you love will reach them – bringing that positive energy home will lift everyone up. It will also show your kids that they should be passionate about things themselves. Before you know it they will have found things they love doing as well and don't be surprised if they take an interest in the thing you love. Your kids want to be just like you. Show them someone great.

Our deepest fear is not that we are inadequate. Our deepest fear is that we are powerful beyond measure. It is our light, not our darkness that most frightens us. We ask ourselves, who am I to be brilliant, gorgeous, talented, fabulous? Actually, who are you not to be? You are a child of God. Your playing it small does not serve the world. There is nothing enlightened about shrinking so that other people won't feel insecure around you. We are all meant to shine, as children do. We were born to make manifest the glory of God that is within us. It is not just in some of us; it is in everyone. And as we let our own light shine, we unconsciously give other people permission to do the same. As we are liberated from our own fear, our presence automatically liberates others.
– Marianne Williamson

HOMEWORK

Make goal setting a priority for yourself in the coming week. Here is how to set and realize a goal:

1. Set aside one hour of uninterrupted time to think about your goal and narrow in on what single thing you want to achieve.
2. Write down your goal.
3. Write down the first step in achieving your goal.
4. Make progress on your goal daily by setting aside time to focus on it. Make your goal a priority.
5. Enjoy the feeling of achievement and satisfaction as you steadily make gains toward what you want.

PRINCIPLE 5 – DO ONE THING AT A TIME

To do two things at once is to do neither.
– Publilius Syrus

Multitasking is overrated. While it's impressive that you might be able to breastfeed, do the dishes, and paint the ceiling at the same time, let's be clear, that is neither the best nor most pleasurable way to do any of those things. Multitasking is a necessary evil but it should never be the goal.

Personally, I am a recovering multitasker. I used to multitask all the time. In the mornings, at the office, all the way up until bedtime. I thought I was being efficient, but I was actually making myself less productive and more stupid. Research shows that constantly switching between tasks or trying to do multiple tasks at once can reduce productivity by up to 40 per cent.[9] Some people have even likened the effects of multitasking to losing a nights sleep or to a 10-point drop in IQ.[10]

Before having kids, I had productivity and IQ points to spare (even though I didn't realize it), so I didn't notice the effects of my

---

[9] "Multitasking: Switching Costs," *American Psychological Association*, March 20, 2006, http://www.apa.org/research/action/multitask.aspx (accessed February 14, 2018).

[10] Peter Bregman, "How and Why to Stop Multitasking," *Harvard Business Review*, May 20, 2010, https://hbr.org/2010/05/how-and-why-to-stop-multitaski.html (accessed February 14, 2018).

multitasking addiction. Fast forward a few years when kids were taking up 212 per cent of my brain capacity and lack of sleep had cut my IQ in half, well, now I had a problem. If I so much as tried to make breakfast and put the dishes away at the same time, I would end up with burnt toast and a clean bowl in the laundry hamper. I had to change my ways. I had to start giving one task at a time my full attention and as I did that, I noticed I was getting more out of each task. I was able to be more mindful of what I was doing and I didn't feel as overwhelmed because I wasn't constantly in the middle of doing five uncompleted tasks.

I even noticed a change in my kids behaviour when I focused on them singularly. When I spoke to them with focus and complete attention – for instance, getting down to their level, looking them in the eye, and explaining things calmly – I got much better results than when I yelled at them from the other room, while simultaneously unloading the dryer, eating my burnt toast, and speaking to their dad on the phone.

Considering how important our time, sleep, and intelligence points are as parents, we simply can't afford to multitask. A good way I have found to prevent myself from getting overwhelmed and to remind myself to focus on one thing at a time is the Ivy Lee Method.[11] Ivy Lee was a public relations professional who, in 1918, met with the president of a steel company and gave him advice on how the company's executives could be more productive. The head of the steel company later paid him $25,000 dollars for the idea (big money back in the day), saying it was the most profitable advice he had ever received. What he told the executive is now called the Ivy Lee Method.

As any parent knows, it can seem nearly impossible to get anything done when you have young kids. Before I started using the Ivy Lee Method, my to-do list was completely overwhelming and it seemed like I could never cross off anything. After one day of using the Ivy Lee Method, I got more checked off than I had done all the previous week (maybe even the previous month).

Simply stated, the method is as follows:

1. Before bed, write down the six most important things you

[11] James Clear, "The Ivy Lee Method: The Daily Routine Experts Recommend for Peak Productivity," *James Clear*, https://jamesclear.com/ivy-lee (accessed February 14, 2018).

need to accomplish the next day. Do not write down more than six.
2. Prioritize those items in order of their importance by numbering them one to six.
3. When you start your tasks the next day, start with number one and work on it until it is complete (or until you have hit a point where you can't complete any more of it) and then start on the second task.
4. Continue through the list in this way until your day is complete.
5. Move any unfinished items to the list for the following day. Always make sure there are only six items on the list and they are prioritized by numbering them one through six.

Such a simple concept. Prioritize your work. Do each task in its proper order until it is completed. Rinse and repeat. So simple, yet few people actually do it, and even if they apply it at work, they almost never apply it at home.

But people aren't idiots. There is a reason they don't do it: our world isn't set up for it. These days the average person is getting bombarded with emails and texts and alerts at all times of the day and night. We aren't compartmentalizing things and taking one task at a time because our attention is constantly being pulled in another direction. What's worse is *we let it.* Rather than limiting our responsiveness or scheduling a time dedicated to responding, we try to get things done in the moment. We "just want to check that one text" while we are the guest of honour at our daughter's tea party and then we wonder why our invite to the next tea party gets lost in the mail and our seat at the table has been taken by a T-rex shaped neck pillow. We shoot off a quick email in aisle six at the grocery store and kick ourselves on the drive home for forgetting the cheddar. By trying to get things done in the moment and not concentrating on the task at hand we do injustice to both things. This was a familiar scenario for me before I started using the Ivy Lee Method:

I'm at home enjoying the weekend. With Sharkey playing happily on her own, I feel compelled to use my free moment productively. I make the mistake of checking my work email on my phone, only to find a message I need to respond to. As I start to craft my reply, Sharkey becomes very interested in the large, non-toddler-friendly cactus in our living room. I lose my focus on the email and call out to Sharkey to leave the cactus. My warning gives her pause for 0.25 seconds and then serves to redouble her interest in the dangerous cactus. I leave my email and sprint across the room to save Sharkey from becoming a pin cushion.

While cursing my pre-child self for even getting an eight-foot cactus, I turn my attention back to my email, only to lose focus again as Sharkey makes another break for the cactus. Now, quite frustrated, I hold Sharkey in one arm to keep her out of trouble, while using the other arm to finish the email. I bounce around the room trying to keep her settled but Sharkey, also quite frustrated, wriggles and pushes to get away from me, pulls my hair and stretches to try to take the phone from my hand.

Things continue to degenerate and I try more and more things to distract Sharkey so I can focus on the email – first the wooden, educational toys, then the flashing, blinking, buzzing toys, and finally my car keys that she is never allowed to play with. It has now taken me over ten minutes to write what should have been a two-minute email, and I'm not even half-way done. As my car alarm blares out through the neighbourhood, I finally admit defeat. My email is in purgatory in my drafts folder. I'm feeling hard-done-by for not even being able to send a simple email and now Sharkey is having a full-blown tantrum because I took the car keys away.

Thankfully, it doesn't have to happen this way. Using the Ivy Lee Method, priorities are clearly laid out for the day so you know exactly what you are going to do. If number one on your list for the day is to spend time with the kids, you shouldn't even be checking emails. You should be giving your kids your full attention – take them to the park, play with them in the yard, build Lego, bake a cake. Whatever it is, it is your time to be with them and not be weighed down by other things. If the number two priority on your list is to get some work done, then you can feel good about taking some time later in the day – after fulfilling your number one priority – to give work your full attention. Because you know these are your priorities in advance you can also set yourself up for success by having someone else be with the kids during your work time or by telling them in advance that you will need to spend an hour working and they will be able to watch TV during that time or whatever it is that works with your circumstance (playdate with a friend, nap time, quiet play etc.). By compartmentalizing the tasks, you are able to give your full attention to each one and get a lot more accomplished in both arenas. You also won't get frustrated by trying to do two competing things and wind up not getting anything out of either of them.

Balancing work and family is always a struggle, but prioritizing your days makes it easier not to compromise on what is important. Being crystal clear in your head about what you want out of your day mitigates the risk of having your day hijacked by activities that aren't a priority for you.

At first, when you start giving one thing your undivided attention, you will find it difficult. Our minds are no longer programmed to concentrate on a single thing at once. It can be uncomfortable and unfamiliar and you might find yourself making excuses. I *have* to reply to that text or I *have* to run out and get milk. Remember, you don't *have* to do anything. Everything you do is your choice. You can choose to do those things or not. You either let those things get in the way of your priorities or you do what you planned to do first and take care of the other things afterwards. If you don't do this for yourself, you will never get to the things that are important to you. Be disciplined and stick to your guns. If you don't have respect for your time, no one else will either.

HOMEWORK

Create your own to-do list using the Ivy Lee Method. To recap, it is as follows:

1. Write down the six most important things you need to accomplish.
2. Number the items from one to six in order of their importance.
3. Start with number one and work on it until it is complete (or until you have hit a point where you can't complete any more of it) and then move on to the second task, and then the third, until the list is complete.

TIP: It isn't always realistic to completely ignore email, phone calls, and texts while plowing through your work in the order of what is most important. Because of that, set yourself up for success by blocking out windows in your day where you will review and respond to those requests, but keep your responsiveness in those pre-set blocks of time. By being responsive all the time we can waste entire days just reacting. Be deliberate with your time; it is a precious resource.

PRINCIPLE 6 – ACCEPT WHAT YOU CAN'T CONTROL

I always feel happy. You know why? Because I never expect anything from anyone.
– William Shakespeare

I stared wide-eyed at my obstetrician.

"Come again?" I said.

"Baby should be here any day now," she said, smiling.

"But I'm not ready!"

Her smile disappeared and her eyebrows raised in concern. "Then you should probably get ready," she said.

As usual, my obstetrician was right. The reality was that I was nine months pregnant with my second child and my new baby boy was ready to make his debut any day. The problem was, I still had things I needed to do to prepare and I wasn't even wrapped up at work yet. Not important things – not in the grand scheme of things – but *things*. Things I had in my head that needed to get done before the baby got here.

First, I wanted to put together the furniture for his room. With my first baby, I had her whole room all set up well in advance and some nights, while I was still pregnant, I would peek in and picture her in there sleeping and I would smile and head off to bed. With the second baby, I was busy with a one year old and a full-time job. When I wasn't working, I was picking up endless toys, falling asleep at 8 pm, or going to the kitchen for tea and then standing there for five minutes trying to remember why I went there in the first place. I felt like I didn't have as much time to lovingly anticipate the arrival of my second baby and I was already feeling guilty that I was treating my second child differently than the first before he was even born. The fact that his furniture was still flat packed on his bedroom floor ate at me, even though I knew it was irrational. He wasn't even going to be in that room for several weeks after arriving because I had a bassinet for him beside my bed. Also, it wasn't like he'd be arriving with luggage he would need to put away, but my pregnant brain had it firmly stuck in there that he simply could not arrive without his dresser and bedside table set up and ready to go.

Next, I wanted to get a manicure and pedicure. One thing I knew from having my first baby is that there isn't a lot you can feel dignified about in the delivery room. I don't know how it is for everyone else, but for me, there seemed to be an unusually high number of people in the delivery room, and I couldn't help but notice I was the only one not wearing pants. Then your body does weird things. Things completely out of your control. You might barf, you might shake, you might grunt, and you will definitely sweat. The one thing you can somewhat reasonably be in control of in the delivery room is your manicure and pedicure. To some people this will sound like the stupidest thing they have ever heard and they will stop reading this book right here and now and immediately write a scathing Amazon review. If you are still with me, try to understand that having manicured fingers and toes was a thin strand of dignity I could clutch while wondering if I had just pooped on a table in front of nine strangers and my husband.

Lastly, I had some errands to run. Errands that would get two pieces of clutter out of the house that had been sitting in the front hall for over a week. I wanted to mail a package to some relatives in England and I wanted to drop off a bag of donations for charity. Again, this was completely irrational, but somehow in my mind those two pieces of clutter were the difference between the baby arriving into a home that was clean, airy, and spacious versus a home that looked like it had been put in a blender.

So there I was. Against a ticking clock. But instead of just accepting the possibility that the baby might arrive before I got everything done, I convinced myself that I could will myself not to go into labour until I decided I was ready.

Over the next two days I was able to wrap up everything at work so I could start my mat leave. On day three, I was free as a bird to get all my things done. *OK, what's first? Furniture. Sure. Should be easy enough for a nine-months-pregnant person to crawl around on the floor putting together some drawers. Dammit. Why don't they just make these things simple? Why does one set of drawers need 956 screws? Hmm... all this handy work is making me hungry. I wonder if we have any apples...*

I waddled my way downstairs to get some apples. Apples were the only thing I craved while I was pregnant. I went through bags and bags of apples. I could never get enough.

OK, back to work, back to work. Allen key, screw number 349... Blurg. I feel weird. Ugh. Why do I feel weird? I'm sure it's nothing. Probably just the apples. I'll just grab another apple and that will settle things down.

Then James appeared in the doorway. Thankfully, the new baby's arrival fell right in between medical school graduation and the start of residency, so James had some time off. "What are you doing? I told you I would put this stuff together this afternoon."

"Yep, I know. I just wanted to do it so I could stand in the doorway and lovingly picture the new baby inside his room. Ummmmm.... I don't feel so great," I said.

James looked concerned. "What do you mean? Is the baby coming? Are you having contractions?"

"Pfft. No. Well, probably not," I said.

James didn't look concerned anymore. He looked like someone who was dealing with an irrational child. He came back at me with science. "If the pains are coming at regular intervals and increasing in intensity and length, they are contractions. Are they happening at regular intervals?"

"I don't know. I'm sure it's nothing. Anyways, I have to get mani-pedi," I said leaving the half-finished drawers on the floor and awkwardly trying to slide past James in the doorway as though I wasn't the width of the doorway itself.

"Right now?" he asked.

"Yes."

"OK, but you should take your phone with you in case you are having contractions," he said as he watched me work my way uncomfortably down the stairs.

"It's not contractions," I called back.

When I arrived at the nail salon, I was still not feeling great and I was angry at James for thinking it could be contractions. *Just some apple indigestion. What does he know about having babies anyway? Oh wonderful. They can see me right away. I'm sure all this discomfort will go away with the warm foot bath. I should really stick to no more than four apples per morning. Yes. That will be my new rule. Oh good, a nice neutral pink for my mani-pedi will be perfect. Yes, that's exactly what I need. It will be so nice and clean-looking. Just like the celebrity moms do for their baby reveal covers.*

Well, since I'm just sitting here I might as well time my episodes of indigestion. Huh, look at that: they're happening just about five minutes apart. Odd.

Omifuckinggawd. OK. It's getting pretty bad. "Just a single coat please. No need for two coats. Nope I won't wait for drying. I will just be very careful. Thanks so much."

Waddling out of the nail salon I finally began wrapping my head around the fact that I was in labour but I was still unwilling to let go of my to-dos.

OK. I'm still fine. Just a couple more errands to get some of this clutter out of the house. I can just mail this package and drop off these donations. Labour lasts such a long time anyway. No need to rush off to the hospital like a madwoman.

Wow. That is a long lineup at the post office. Maybe I shouldn't wait. I mean, what if my water breaks or something? That would be super embarrassing. What if I leave now and my water breaks in the car? Can you get that out of a car or will it ruin the car forever? Maybe I should get myself some Depends at the drug store in case my water breaks. Oh, never mind that. The line is moving. Good. But it's still really long. Maybe I'm being unreasonable. I should go. Normal people don't wait to mail packages while they are in labour. I should be normal and leave. Buuuut… the line isn't that long and I've already been waiting… yes, I can wait. I want this done. If I don't do it now, the baby will arrive into all this clutter and it will be terrible. No trouble. I can wait. I can wait.

*Grrrrrrrrr… What the HECK is taking so long? Why is that stupid woman still at the counter? Just MAIL YOUR PACKAGE LADY. I will pay for the freaking tracking if you just SPEED THE EF UP. Some of us are in labour over here and trying to get all their sh*t done so their baby can have a nice life. OK, calm down. Breathe. No wait, hold your breath. Yeah, that's better. OK. I'm third in line. I can do this. I can do this.*

The woman in front of me turned around, looked at me in the kindest way she could possibly look at a certifiably crazy person and said, "I know what's happening and I think you should go ahead of me." What does she mean she knows what is happening? Does everyone know what is happening? I just found out what is happening. I also thought I was being super stealth. Is it the sweat? Am I sweating? I mean, yes, I'm wearing a T-shirt and flip flops in January in Canada but maybe I just run hot. Did I grunt? Am I making noises? How does she know? Oh good, I'm up.

OK, package is mailed. Contractions are getting closer together. But what about the donations? I need this clutter out of the house so my baby doesn't have to live in squalor. Uuuuuggggggghhhhhhh. Why do contractions hurt so much? Why is labour so hard? Why is this all happening on a Saturday when everything is so busy? Oooh, are those apples? Never mind the apples. Home, home, home. Must get home. Maybe we can stop off at the donations place on the way to the hospital. Yes, that will be perfect. It's almost right on the way. Uuuuuggggggghhhhhhh.

I stormed into the house as fast as a nine-months-pregnant person can storm anywhere.

I called out to James, "James, we have to go to the hospital and we have to drop off some donations."

Being a nice man, James ignored my donations comment and focused on the fact that I was in labour. "OK, I will call the hospital and you call your mom to come watch Sharkey."

When I called my mom, she was in the shower. Thankfully she had brought the phone into the shower with her in case I went into labour. At least one of us was thinking rationally.

"Mom, you have to come watch Sharkey because the baby is coming," I said while I hung myself over the back of the couch to try to manage the pain.

My mom responded with a reasonable sense of urgency seeing as labours generally take several hours to progress. "Oh! OK. I will just rinse my hair and dry it and be right over."

"No, no time. You have to come right now," I groaned.

My mom was surprised seeing as she lived just 20 minutes away. "What? Really? Why didn't you call me earlier?"

"I had to do some errands."

In the end, we didn't drop off the donations on the way to the hospital. Our new baby, who we named Jack, was born just a couple hours after we got to the hospital and when we brought him home the next day, he didn't seem the least bit fazed by the bag of donations still sitting by the front door. He did seem pleased with his room though. Thankfully, James had finished putting together the furniture while I was out running errands, just as he said he would.

What I learned, all too late, was that if I had simply accepted the fact that I was not going to be able to control everything leading up to Jack's birth, I could have made that day a lot easier on myself. When we try to control things that are outside of our control, it can lead to stress and frustration. But if we accept that there are things we can't control and then move forward with that understanding, things can be much more pleasant overall.

But for some reason, as humans, we struggle to accept circumstances that aren't what we expect or aren't what we want. Before meeting me, my husband was in the military. His training was very intense physically, but one of the most challenging aspects was what they described as "dislocation of expectations." This was a technique they used to build mental toughness. It was telling the trainees one thing would happen and then they would do the opposite. For instance, after a really tough day of training, they might tell the trainees that they will get to sleep in the next day until 7 am but then they will wake them up at 3 am to run through exercises in the cold mud. Or they might tell them to clean their weapons thoroughly and then, after spending all the time to do a good job, they would tell them to do it again.

It could be argued that being a parent is one long exercise in mental toughness. Kids are always dislocating expectations because they come with a lot of uncontrolled variables right from the get-go. Boy or girl, delivery date, size, temperament. None of those things can be preselected or controlled and some people feel that lack of control significantly.

These days we are able to control so many things that the majority of us struggle when we encounter something we cannot. We decide when and what to eat. If you want a banana in the dead of winter in Saskatchewan, Canada, all you need to do is shell out the 59 cents. We decide the temperature of our homes and argue over it with our spouses to the degree. We decide what to watch on TV, the colour of our hair, the timing of our vacations. Having children is one of the few things we have no control over, yet we still try.

We want to know everything and plan everything, often starting before the child is even born. As expectant parents we get special apps to see how our babies are developing and what fruit they most closely resemble. We read parenting books and attend classes, we consult with doctors and midwives and talk to friends and family who have children already. Some of us have detailed birth plans and ideas in our heads about what being a mom or dad will be like in those first days. How we will feel and how our baby will act. We have plans to follow a particular parenting style or set of theories when raising our children. Everything from ideas about how to discipline to how to guarantee they will love broccoli.

Naturally, we idealize these scenarios. We picture everything going exactly to plan. Expert A tells us to follow simple sure-fire steps to having a broccoli-loving child. Eat plenty of broccoli while pregnant. Make yourself broccoli smoothies while breastfeeding and make broccoli one of the first five foods introduced to your infant and you will have a broccoli lover for life. You followed Expert A's advice to a T, so why is your little angel spitting broccoli out in your face? What happens when things don't go to plan? We could fight it, making broccoli in new and exciting ways for breakfast, lunch, and dinner, buying better and brighter ergonomic spoons, and introducing new airplane noises for each meal, or we could accept that our little one doesn't feel like broccoli at the moment and try again in a week or two.

It's the people and parents who can adapt to new and unplanned circumstances who will be happiest. Did you think your baby would be perfect? That they would sleep through the night, happily keep sunglasses and hats on their head, and not poop all over Nana at her 95th birthday party? Did you think you would be great at being a parent? That you would have time to dress your baby in clothes with buttons, be able to exercise calm and patience at all times, and never accidentally answer the door with one breast out? That is fantastic. If this happens for you, I am genuinely impressed and happy for you. If it doesn't happen for you, it's OK. Don't beat yourself up or try to fight reality. Adapt to the current scenario. Try to see things as they truly are and move forward from that point.

I look for the best and am prepared for the opposite.
– Seneca

When we have a child, we go from being responsible for one person to being responsible for two. It puts new exterior forces on your life. You no longer have the freedom you did before having children because you are now responsible for someone else's wellbeing too. And while we are the only people who are in control of ourselves, we are not in control of, nor can we control, our children. If you doubt this, take a moment to call your mom and ask her how "in control" she felt while you were a teenager.

Of course, this extends to our spouse, and then to our family and friends. We can't expect our children, spouse, or family and friends to act exactly as we would like them to. We can't expect our kids will never cry or will sleep when we want them to, we can't expect our spouse to interact with the child exactly as we want them to or when we want them to, and we can't expect our family and friends to help in the way we want them to. To have general positive expectations in life is good. To expect specific behaviours from specific people is asking for disappointment.

Some mourn the loss of freedom that comes with having children, and feel that lack of control much more acutely, but the truth is, as a parent you have just as much control as you always did. We are all still only in control of ourselves, just as we were before children, and being in control of yourself means you are in control of how you react to the world. When your baby cries, do your best to soothe them but if they cannot be soothed right away, don't blame yourself. If your spouse is interacting with the baby in a way you don't like, leave them be. It is their child, too, and they need to establish their own relationship. Sometimes friends and family can think they are helping when they are actually making it more difficult for you. Either tell them how they can help you specifically, or take their good intentions for what they are and be appreciative of the effort.

The worst thing you can do for yourself is dwell on how you wanted things to be different. You will make yourself unhappy and sick. Instead, take a step back, take stock of where you are, focus on the good, forgive the bad, and keep going.

Remember, we can and should expect great things from ourselves but we can not and should not expect things from others. You do yourself a disservice when you give other people control over your happiness. What other people do around you should not determine whether you are happy or not, whether you have a good day or a bad day. The only person in control of your feelings and how you react to your circumstances, is you. If your happiness is dependent on the actions of others, you are putting yourself at great risk of unhappiness.

As you go through your day try to actively protect your mood from being trampled on by things that are out of your control. There's no more of your favourite almond milk at the store? You'll live. Traffic terrible on the way home? Getting angry won't get you there faster. Baby won't nap? OK, that's pretty bad but try not to let it ruin the rest of your day. If you are intentional with your mood each day and work on catching yourself in the moment, you can prevent yourself from getting into a negative headspace. Try to see things for what they are, accept the circumstances, and move forward from there. As you do this more and more, it will be easier and easier to do.

A common scenario might happen when your baby is very young. In these early days, one person is often home with the baby while the other is at work. As diapers and fatigue pile up throughout the day, that person often starts longing for a break. A moment to themselves to sleep or eat or stare into space. They start picturing what they will do when their partner comes home. They imagine immediately handing the baby off so they can finally have two hands free to open a jar of olives or put on socks. Yes, that will be bliss. They will get some reprieve at 5:43 pm. They will immediately hand off the baby and then they will be so happy just to eat olives and put on socks. Then maybe they can sit and read or just stare into space for a few minutes while the baby is being cared for by someone else.

But what happens when they get a text at 5:30 pm saying a client meeting has run late and there is an evening conference call that needs to happen? What happens when there is no reprieve, olives, socks, or staring into space? Because the person has been daydreaming about this all day, they are disappointed, angry, resentful. They were counting on someone else for their happiness and when that plan went sideways, so did their happiness.

As I mentioned, when I had my first baby, I was on my own for big chunks of time while my husband was working out of town. As I interacted with other moms at coffee shops, parks and baby classes, I realized that even though I had less help than a lot of other moms with young babies, I seemed to be happier. That was curious to me and I started to think about it a lot. I wasn't any different from these ladies. Sharkey was a great baby, but I had no child experience and I was under the same stresses as many of the other moms with sleep and crying. I could tell having a positive attitude was a large part of it, but I also noticed that, because I wasn't expecting anyone to come and help, I had to figure out how to make it work on my own. I felt a great sense of accomplishment when I did something on my own that other people often needed help with. If my parents or a friend showed up to help out, that was a wonderful bonus. My friends with kids the same age would always comment that they didn't know how I was doing this on my own but, interestingly, it was partly because I was doing it on my own that I was so happy.

Don't get me wrong – I love my husband and I would much rather have had him closer to home and he would have rather been there as well. I am certainly not suggesting people should start single parenting in order to be happy, nor am I downplaying the difficulty of single parenting – but because I wasn't expecting a break or expecting someone to come help, I was not vulnerable to that expectation going south. I was in control of my own circumstances and I was responsible for my own outcomes.

With our second baby, my husband was working closer to home, but I tried to maintain the same attitude that had worked so well for me the first time. Even if James was supposed to be home at a certain time, I would try not to have any expectations about how that would go. I would not center my day around the moment he got home, thinking of what I would do once he was able to take over child-minding. I would plan to do whatever needed to be done with the kids and if he was able to take on some of it when he got home, that was wonderful, but never expected. It served me well because that way whenever he had to work late or leave early or had paperwork he needed to get to at home, it wouldn't blow up plans I had made for myself. It was a great freedom to be in control of my own time and tasks.

This leads to one of the key elements of not having expectations of others and, in my opinion, one of the key elements of being happy: do things for yourself.

Chop your own wood and it will warm you twice.
– Henry Ford

It's easy to get caught up in one's expectations of what others will do and how they will do it, and these expectations are often derailed, especially between couples. This can create a lot of angst that "he" or "she" didn't do something, which causes problems within the couple and a lot of unnecessary stress. Take the following example.

I was at my friend's house one day and she went to throw something in the garbage, only to find it was full. She smacked her forehead. "Argh! I asked him to take this out!" She then started in on a familiar tirade about her husband and how he never does anything to help out around the house. I looked at her husband who was outside talking to one of their kids. "Why don't you just take out the garbage yourself?" I asked. "Because I am always doing everything and I am sick of it." "OK. Then if you asked him to do it, just forget about the garbage and he will take it out in his own time." My friend was no longer listening. She turned away and continued muttering about her husband under her breath. I looked again at her husband out the window. The full garbage was clearly not weighing on him in the way it was weighing on her. A few short minutes later, he came in silently, unaware of the conversation that had just taken place, grabbed the garbage and headed to the bins outside. Even though the task was now done, my friend was still fuming over the whole thing and her husband probably had no clue as to why she was so angry.

Observing the two of them in this incident, it was crystal clear that the true victim in this scenario was my friend. She was staking her happiness on her husband's actions, and when the task wasn't done exactly as she wanted, she was furious. If she had just taken out the garbage herself when she initially noticed it was full she wouldn't be wasting her mental and emotional energy on something as meaningless as garbage.

It is very important to note here that this very familiar scenario may not be about the garbage and that a larger issue needs to be addressed. My friend said the work balance in the household was off. Now, hear me out. If we look at the cold hard facts, having an imbalance in household chores is going to be the case in 100 per cent of households. Nothing is ever going to be perfectly even and there is no way of possibly measuring household tasks evenly. Are three diaper changes equal to one garage being swept out? Is a grocery run equal to two hours of work at the office? If you take the kids is it three? If I walk the dog, are you making dinner? Trying to make everything perfectly even will drive a person crazy. Two people, actually. What is important is that the people living in the household feel there is a fair balance between them. A balance both parties are happy with. No two circumstances are going to be exactly alike. Personally, I find that when you look at another family's circumstances, you often wonder how they could ever live like that. I can't name one person in this world with whom I would change situations, and you may feel the same looking around at the situations of your friends and families. Thankfully, you don't need to live like that – only they do. You need to live with your own circumstances, so if someone in the house is unhappy with the balance of work, then you need to talk to one another about it so you can solve the problem. Taking a stand at the garbage bin is not going to solve the larger issue and it will only cause additional frustration. Work it out so everyone can feel good.

Assuming there are no larger issues about the balance of work in the household, if something needs to be done, do it. Especially if it is something that is going to take only a few minutes. If you do little things as you go, fewer things pile up and you'll find you have more time in your day than you think. And checking something off your list will make you feel good, or at the very least, will prevent it from being a point of frustration for you.

When I was off work and home with the kids, I would try my best not to make a mental list of chores for James to do once he walked in the door. If there were chores I could do – even if they were something James would typically have done – I would try to do them. Tighten screws on a door hinge, change batteries in a toy, mouse-proof the pantry, change lightbulbs. Of course there were things that weren't realistic to do while I was watching the children or that I just didn't get to during the day, and James was always willing to do things, too, but by taking responsibility for doing all those little things, I was much happier, because I felt in control.

By waiting for others to do things for us we are robbing ourselves of the opportunity to be happy now. Simply getting things done takes a lot less mental energy than dwelling and stewing about them all day. Do for yourself and be happier.

I recently tried to teach my daughter this lesson when she asked me to do up the seatbelt on her car seat for her. "Sharkey," I said in my best authoritative voice. "You should do up your own seatbelt because doing things for yourself will make you a happier person."

"No it doesn't," she responded matter-of-factly. "I'm happier when you do it."

We will keep working on it.

HOMEWORK

Assignment A: Take a few minutes to think about some issues that trigger frustration for you. Try to see them in a new light, to see them for what they are. Be honest with yourself about whether or not there is anything you are able to change about those situations, or if you simply need to accept them as they are and move forward from there.

Assignment B: If there is something you have been putting off, waiting for someone else to do it, go do it right now.

PRINCIPLE 7 – GIVE YOUR FULL EFFORT

If you want to achieve excellence, you can get there today. As of this second, quit doing less-than-excellent work.
– Thomas J. Watson

The year my son was born was a big year for us. James had finished medical school and had been offered a three-year residency in a small ski village in Maine, U.S.A. Up until this point of his schooling, I had stayed in our home town of Toronto, Canada, while he went abroad to medical school and for his internships. This was partly so I could work (medical school is expensive) and partly for my sanity (most of my friends and family were in Toronto and I love the city).

But now things were a lot different than when he started medical school. For one, we now had two kids who presumably wanted their dad to be a real live person, not a talking head on an iPad. For another, if we all moved to the small ski village, the cost of living would be much lower and I could stay home with the kids. Although I found my work rewarding, this was really appealing to me because I enjoyed being home with the kids during my maternity leaves far more than I ever thought I would. Also, in the time I had been at work and caring for Sharkey, I had found it really challenging to be both the professional and the parent I wanted to be – and that was when I only had one child. Now that there were two kids, I didn't feel confident about what I would be able to provide in both arenas. Also, James was about to be working incredibly long and irregular hours as a resident, so having at least one stable, available parent was something I wanted for the kids.

So that's what we did. We packed up and moved to this beautiful, picturesque little town. My parents helped us with the move and when they left, they cried. Not because they were happy for me and not because they would miss us. They cried because they thought I wouldn't be able to handle living in a small town, essentially on my own with two kids, while James was working all the time.

As usual, my parents were right. My new life was extremely challenging, but not for the reasons they thought. They thought I wouldn't be able to handle small-town life but I was actually doing pretty well at that part. I got used to the only coffee shop in town opening whenever they pleased, not when I pleased. I understood that people knew who I was even though I didn't know who they were, and I even successfully navigated a conversation on pig castration (at least I think I did). The part of my new life that I was finding challenging was being a full-time, stay-at-home mom.

You know those people who love cleaning out their refrigerators, spend three days making home-made croissants, and who don't simply stack things to "tidy up"? I'm not one of those people. My grandmother was one of those people. She genuinely enjoyed caring for her home and the people in it. Once, when we were there for dinner, I tried to help her with the dishes but she stopped me at the sink. "Please don't," she said. "Don't take away my fun." She was a wonderful and magical creature, but wonder and magic are not traits that are passed down genetically, so I gladly stepped aside, leaving her to her "fun." Another time, after my grandmother had passed away, my sister and I unknowingly both used my grandmother's chocolate chip cookie recipe to make cookies for my parents at Christmas. My sisters cookies were perfect circles wrapped in perfectly folded tissue inside a beautiful green box with a matching bow. Mine were misshapen and gifted in a reused cookie tin lined with wax paper. It was actually funny (and not a little embarrassing) to see the two gifts beside one another.

Perhaps because of my domestic challenges, I had never really mentally committed to being a full-time, stay-at-home mom. Even though I had a year-long maternity leave with my first baby, I always thought of myself as an executive who was temporarily home with the kids; because I never thought of being a stay-at-home mom as my primary job, I gave myself a pass on the fact that I wasn't very good at it. I never tried hard at any of the domestic things that are associated with being a stay-at-home mom. I didn't think I had to. In my mind, it was OK that I wasn't good at cleaning up after meals, folding laundry, or cleaning under my kids' fingernails, because I was good at planning budgets, project management, and drafting reports. But now that being home with the kids was my full-time and only gig, serving peanut butter and jam sandwiches for dinner just didn't feel right. I needed to do better at this job. I needed to find a way to enjoy domestic activities, so I could teach my kids important life lessons about cleaning up after yourself, keeping a tidy home, and making personal hygiene and healthy eating a priority.

But how? How does one make washing the dishes and folding laundry fun when you are not a wonderful and magical creature? I thought back to when I would work on accounts that weren't inherently interesting to me, and I realized that when you try hard at the work, the content doesn't matter as much. When you put in genuine effort, you feel rewarded no matter what the task is. So, I decided to try out this method out with my new job to see if I could get satisfaction from homemaking by giving it my full effort.

Over the coming weeks I tried much harder at my domestic chores and, amazingly, I found I was getting more satisfaction out of them. I really liked seeing all the laundry lined up in the drawers and I started to enjoy looking for and preparing recipes that were simple but tasty. I still hated doing dishes and tidying up, so I would set myself a 15-minute timer to see how much I could get through in that amount of time, which, to my great relief, was a lot! To be clear, my house was by no means at a Marie Kondo level of cleanliness and organization, but it was a lot better than it had been when I was giving no effort or half an effort.

A few weeks later, I was feeling pretty good about myself as I sat down at the table admiring my healthy, homemade dinner. In sharp contrast, I noticed Sharkey and Jack both frowning and looking deflated.

"What's up, guys?" I asked.

Due to Jack's limited vocabulary at the time, Sharkey would often speak for both of them: "Jack and I wanted peanut butter and jam for dinner." Sadly, effort is not always appreciated.

When I was a teenager, my dad would pull out the old adage, "If something is worth doing, it is worth doing right." I was at the receiving end of that sentence countless times. It usually came when I just needed to get something done quickly – a project that was due the following day or something I wanted a quick answer to – but I never got a quick fix from my dad. I got a thought-out plan of action and several ways I could make whatever it was that I was doing even better. With additional effort and time, of course.

I was endlessly frustrated by this as a teenager but I eventually came to appreciate it. It turns out the most rewarding tasks in life are the ones you are fully committed to and the ones you *really* try at. Things in life are not automatically meaningful. Things are given meaning when we give them our time and attention. That's where you find the real value in life. You can call it being fully committed, gaining mastery, or being all-in, but whatever you call it, it is the complete giving of yourself to something or someone without expecting anything to come back to you in return.

I once received training on how to be all-in with clients. The trainer laid out the difference between being all-in and not. The person who is not all-in goes through the motions of their working day. They get things checked off their list, they fulfill the role of their job without going beyond it, and the work doesn't mean much to them. They are doing the job but they aren't fully committed to doing it to the absolute best of their ability. They are following the proper steps to get things accomplished, but are not improving on their work, or giving the work their own added style.

The all-in person is living very much by my dad's philosophy of "if it's worth doing, it's worth doing right." They are thinking of ways to make improvements to every part of their day and every aspect of their job. The trainer gave us examples of people who were all-in: for instance, a person who would hand-deliver their client's invoice each month and review it with them so they knew exactly what they were getting for their money. Another example was a person who would keep track of the important events in her client's life – things like her son's baseball game or birthdays – and would make sure not to bug her about work during those times. The all-in person isn't just good at their job, they are *great* at it.

Many of my colleagues who attended the session came away with to-do lists taken from the trainer's examples of ways to go above and beyond with clients, but I think those colleagues missed the point. Being all-in isn't about checking things off a to-do list, but about being passionate about your work and treating the people you work with like human beings, not check marks on a project timeline. It is about putting in effort where it makes the most sense to do so and being committed to doing the best job you can do, not copying what others are doing. Being all-in is a frame of mind.

When I think about being all-in, I am reminded of a time I was taking my small dog for a walk and out of nowhere she tensed up and the hair on her neck and back stood up. She squared herself to something over to the right of us and started growling like I had never heard her do before. I looked over and there was a life-sized bronze statue of a bull that my Jack Russel Pug was about to throw down with. I thought two things in that moment. One, maybe the dog's eyesight isn't great, and two, if that were a real bull, I think it would have backed down. My 17-pound dog was so committed to this fight that I don't think the bull would have risked it. That is the kind of commitment and energy you want to channel to get the most out of life.

Attack each day with an enthusiasm unknown to mankind.
– Jim Harbaugh

Completely committing to something shouldn't be confused with being the best at something. Being fully committed is giving your best effort and best self to a situation, and doing things with intention. It doesn't matter how that compares to how others are doing. So often we look at others and compare ourselves to them, especially as parents. What others are doing doesn't matter. It has no impact on your family. Don't spend your energy trying to emulate others or beating yourself up for not doing better. You will never be able to be true to yourself while trying to be someone else. Spend that energy being the best version of yourself that you can be. I guarantee your best is more than enough.

Completely committing to something also doesn't mean spending the most time. Sometimes doing things well will take time, but time put in doesn't automatically equal a great output. If we spend time without deliberation and reflection it could be wasted time. As we've discussed, distracted time is usually ineffective time.

There are also times when taking a break is the best way to address a situation. In the early days of having kids, parents are rarely getting the sleep they need, but if they get a free minute, they feel they have to tidy up or catch up on emails – anything other than take a minute for themselves to rest, sleep, or stare into space. The dishes and vacuuming and everything else can wait. You will be more productive later if you take a break and get the rest you need. You can live with a dirty floor. You can't live without sleep.

Like time, another thing that can be confused with commitment is spending money. As parents we want to give our kids the best, but the best isn't always stuff. We get drawn in by countless gadgets and toys for brain building and motor development. Or we feel guilty about not spending more time with our kids, so we replace that time with gifts. Or we feign interest in something by throwing money at it rather than taking an active part in it. I know one mom who brags about getting her son all the best hockey equipment, but she has never been to a single one of his games.

Opportunity is missed by most people because it is dressed in overalls and looks like work.
– Thomas Edison

You might be wondering, if being fully committed is so rewarding, why don't more people do it? There are two possible answers. The first is that it takes effort. When there are so many things happening, many people just need to get things done fast, they don't feel they have time to do things in the best way possible. But remember, being committed doesn't necessarily mean you have to spend more time or meet a Martha Stewart standard of home life but you do have to be committed to doing *your* best. Your real best – not your good-enough best – and once you've done your best, you need to be OK with that level of achievement, even if it doesn't match the level of your sister or your mother-in-law or that superdad three doors down. Be proud of what *you* do and forget what others are doing.

The other reason people don't fully commit to kicking the pants out of their home life is because, at some level, they are worried that if they try, they will fail. But guess what? If you don't try, you fail anyway. You might as well aim high and see what you can get out of life.

The first time I genuinely gave a home-life activity my all was when my daughter was just a few weeks old. Since James was away for long stretches with work, I was caring for our daughter and two dogs on my own for the majority of the time. I was new to the whole baby thing and still learning to balance feeding, sleeping and pooping with getting outside – and I had to get outside in order to walk the dogs.

On one hand, I felt like I had an excuse to not take the dogs out – I had a new baby, I was on my own, and it was winter. Also, one of the dogs was 130 pounds. Walking him on his own was sometimes a challenge. On the other hand, I was on maternity leave and had 24 hours each day to make sure the baby and the two dogs were fed, changed, walked, and breathing. Even if it took me all 24 hours of the day, I was going to make it happen.

I had an infant insert in our baby carrier, so I could wear the baby in the carrier on my front, put my winter coat around both of us, take one dog's leash in each hand, and set off. Theoretically. Here was the actual process:

Feed the baby, make sure she doesn't fall asleep before getting in the carrier, make sure her diaper is clean, and put her into an undershirt and warm, footed sleeper. Make sure I am wearing clothes I can go outside in (i.e. my "nice" sweats). Put the baby someplace safe while I get the dogs ready. Put the dogs' leashes on and any necessary outerwear, depending on the weather. Drape the ends of the dog leashes over the back of the chair so I can grab them after I get the baby and my coat on. Put my boots on (if this step was forgotten, I would need to wear slip-on summer shoes, because I couldn't reach my feet once the baby was on me). Put the baby into the newborn insert and front carrier and make sure she is secure and happy. Realize baby has a soiled diaper. Take everything off, change baby, and get back to the same point in the getting-ready process. Put hat on baby. Put coat on me and baby. Put hat on me. Get mitts and put them in my pockets so I can take them out after locking the door behind me. Notice the dog leashes have fallen from the back of the chair. Curse life itself. Do a crazy backbend to try to find the dog leashes on the floor. Arrange the dogs so there is one in each hand. Exit the house, lock the door, put on mitts, and GO!

At first, my dog walks would take me ages. Sometimes it took longer to get everyone ready than we spent on the walk. But after a little while, I was getting pretty good at keeping everyone fed, walked, and alive, so I was able to add more things to my plate. Longer walks, going out to see friends, grocery shopping, mom and baby yoga, starting photo albums, baking misshapen cookies, learning to knit, and so on. I started to feel like I was getting the most out of my time on maternity leave and I felt really good about it.

I slept and dreamt that life was joy. I awoke and saw that life was service. I acted and behold, service was joy.
– Rabindranath Tagore

With each new thing I was able to do on my own, I felt a sense of accomplishment. And I got excited about my next challenge. These challenges may not seem like much to some people, but to others, they are big hills to climb. It is completely up to the individual, as only they know what will be a worthwhile challenge. Many new parents feel housebound in the early days of having kids; it can be a daunting task to get kids ready to go, and navigating something like grocery shopping can be a delicate balance of feeding, diapering, and controlling fussiness. Some parents decide to opt out and say they simply can't grocery shop with kids and they arrange it so one person stays with the baby and one person does the shopping. Dividing tasks or cutting down on activities you know are going to be frustrating makes sense, but be careful what you become paralyzed by. You are capable of more than you think. Because I was on my own for so much of the time, I needed to be able to do everything with the baby in tow. The unexpected benefit was doing everything on my own made me feel great. I learned I could leave the house any time I wanted to and I would be OK. I could run errands with the baby strapped to me. I could visit friends or family or take a walk with just me and the baby to clear my head and get some much-needed fresh air for both of us. By trying new things and not limiting your thinking, you find your world is much more open that you ever thought possible.

As you work on giving life your full effort you will start to notice amazing changes in how you see yourself and your world. Life is so much better when you are working hard and doing things to the best of your ability. If you find you are slipping back into the same old habits and ways of thinking, refocus and start again with renewed effort and energy.

As you go through your days, remember that an all-in mindset isn't about being someone else's version of all-in, but about being your own version of all-in. I can't take the things the all-in trainer told me and apply them to every client because those gestures would be insincere and they would come across that way. It is the same with home life. What works for one person won't work for another. Being all-in is a mindset, not a checklist. Do things with intention. Don't let life happen to you. Take your life where you want it to go.

Perfection is not attainable, but if we chase perfection
we can catch excellence.
– Vince Lombardi

HOMEWORK

Decide in this moment that you are going to try really, really hard at life and you are going to keep trying hard for one month. Give life your very best effort. At work, give more than what you are paid for. At home, give as much of yourself as you can to your family. If you have a hobby or interest give full effort to that as well. If you've been putting off something you have always wanted to do, start your first step this month. Don't wait until tomorrow. Do it now.

Go through each day intentionally, thinking about how you want to do things and what you want to get out of them. Understand you are capable of much more than you think. Get energized about the things you do. Take responsibility for yourself. Start new routines and habits that you enjoy. Be the person you want to be.

Use this template to start your commitment and get focused.

I, ____________________, started my All-in Challenge on ____________________. As part of this challenge, I will commit to doing the following:

1.
2.
3.

My first step for each of the above will be:

1.
2.
3.

PRINCIPLE 8 – APPRECIATE WHAT YOU HAVE

We tend to forget that happiness doesn't come as a result of getting something we don't have, but rather of recognizing and appreciating what we do have.
– Frederick Keonig

In a world of carefully cultivated Facebook feeds and filtered Instagram photos it can be easy to get down on the realities of one's own life. It can be hard not to compare ourselves to others; unfortunately, we aren't usually thinking, "Look at me living my best life!" but something more along the lines of "Damn, I wish I could spend time with painting elephants," or "Damn, I wish my whole family would look at the camera at the same time," or "Damn, I wish I could wear pants with a waistband."

A few months after moving to the U.S., I found myself in a bit of a funk. My Facebook feed was filled with comments about people getting ready for Canadian Thanksgiving and I was feeling sorry for myself because I was away from my family and James had to work all of Thanksgiving weekend. I decided to skip Thanksgiving all together, since the kids were too young to know any different. There was no point in making a Turkey. Jack was barely eating solids and Sharkey and I wouldn't make much of a dent in a full Thanksgiving meal. I figured it would just be a waste.

The day before Thanksgiving, the kids and I were in the grocery store getting normal, non-Thanksgiving meal items when a woman stopped us. "You are so lucky," she said to me with a big smile. "Such a beautiful family. Mine are all grown up. I miss this age. I mean, yes, it's tiring and busy but it's such a wonderful and special time. Enjoy it." As she looked happily at me and the kids, I could tell she was thinking of her own children and the special memories she had of them when they were little. I felt like a total jackass. Here I was, ready to forget Thanksgiving entirely – literally, the time of year when you are meant to be thankful for all that you have – when I had the two cutest humans in the world to share it with. I mean, their poor dad had to work and he wasn't complaining. What was wrong with me?

So we changed tack. We still couldn't eat a whole turkey, but I bought a turkey breast and I picked up all the traditional sides to go with it (pies, mostly). It was still way too much food for one full-sized person and two half-sized persons, so I decided we could eat some ourselves and then take the rest to James at work so he could enjoy a taste of Thanksgiving as well. He then shared it with a colleague who was away from family as well, so even more good came of it.

When I stopped focusing on what I didn't have and started appreciating what I did have, I was able to enjoy one of my favourite Thanksgivings ever. It didn't feature the best food or the most people or the nicest decorations but it reminded me how much there was to be thankful for.

We all know it's good to be grateful for what we have, but did you know it can make you happier? Studies have shown that gratitude is associated with greater happiness, including feeling more positive emotions, relishing good experiences, improving health, dealing with adversity, and building strong relationships.[12] The simple act of being thankful can make you a happier, healthier person.

In addition, one of the most important things gratitude does is focus your attention on the good happening in your life *now*. Sometimes people get into the nasty habit of waiting for something else to happen before they can be happy. They might be waiting until they finish school, then waiting for a better job, then for a different

[12] "Giving Thanks Can Make You Happier," *Harvard Health Publishing*, https://www.health.harvard.edu/healthbeat/giving-thanks-can-make-you-happier (accessed February 14, 2018).

house or more money. People wait until they have more time, waiting for their kids to start school or waiting until things aren't as busy. Then maybe they wait for their kids to be out of the house, for retirement.

You can get so confused
that you'll start in to race
down long wiggled roads at a break-necking pace
and grind on for miles cross weirdish wild space,
headed, I fear, toward a most useless place.
The Waiting Place…

…for people just waiting.
Waiting for a train to go
or a bus to come, or a plane to go
or the mail to come, or the rain to go
or the phone to ring, or the snow to snow
or waiting around for a Yes or a No
or waiting for their hair to grow.
Everyone is just waiting.

Waiting for the fish to bite
or waiting for wind to fly a kite
or waiting around for Friday night
or waiting perhaps for their Uncle Jake
or a pot to boil, or a Better Break
or a string of pearls, or a pair of pants
or a wig with curls, or Another Chance.

Everyone is just waiting.

Excerpt from Oh The Places You'll Go! By Dr. Seuss

Without even realizing it, a whole lifetime could pass while you wait for what's next. The tragedy in this circumstance is twofold: you may never do the things you have been waiting to do, and you won't have properly appreciated the journey because your gaze was always fixed on the next thing, instead of the good things happening right now. Being grateful focuses our attention on what we do have rather than what we will have. It makes what we have in the moment enough for us to be happy.

Some people seem to be grateful naturally. These people are easy to find. They are usually happy and surrounded by people who love being around them. If you are not in that fortunate group, you need to put energy into training your brain to see the good in life. Luckily there are simple ways to change your outlook to be more thankful for the things you have.

First, you can change the way you speak about things. Fitness professional and author Ben Bergeron encourages people to "turn every 'have-to' into 'get-to.'" So you don't *have* to put your kids to bed tonight, you *get* to put your kids to bed tonight. You don't *have* to work out, you *get* to work out. You don't *have* to meet your parents for dinner, you *get* to meet your parents for dinner. Changing the way you refer to things will shift your thinking around them and you will almost instantly feel more thankful and positive about the things you do in your day.

Next, if you catch yourself dwelling on negative things that can't be reframed using the above method, pause and think about three things you are thankful for or are wonderful in your life. As parents, we are lucky. We have built in miracles in our lives that we can be grateful for everyday (even if they are the source of frustration at that same moment). Even without kids it shouldn't be hard to find three. We can be thankful to have a home, thankful for our friends and family, thankful for pets. We also can and should be thankful for the little things in life: a sunny day, a favourite sweater, a hot coffee.

Whenever I was challenged by the early days of child-rearing I would think of a less appealing alternative situation to remind myself that life was actually pretty great in the larger scheme of things. If the baby were crying I would remind myself that some people never get to have children at all. If the baby was being very demanding I would remind myself that if I were not at home caring for her, I could very possibly be in a nightmare meeting with a demanding client. At least the demanding baby was cute! Naturally, what each person is thankful for will be different, and sometimes the thing we are most grateful for as parents is a break, but coming up with less appealing alternatives always made me feel thankful for the circumstance I was in, even when that circumstance was trying.

Some people grumble that roses have thorns; I am grateful that thorns have roses.
– Alphonse Karr

The final way to change your outlook is to set aside time in your day to reflect on the same thing mentioned above. Pick three things to be thankful or grateful for and either write them down each day or say them aloud to yourself. Book it in your calendar, set an alarm, or do it first thing in the morning or last thing at night. It doesn't matter when you do it but you need to make sure it doesn't get forgotten.

Our brains are plastic and what we do each day with our minds shapes how they interpret the world. We can build happy brains but we need to put the right effort and energy into doing it. We need to exercise our brains in the right way. You can consider it your happiness workout.

HOMEWORK

Take a few minutes to be thankful for what you have. Aim to fill up one full sheet of paper with things you are thankful for. As parents, half the page might be filled simply by listing things we are thankful for that relate to our kids and our families. Be thankful for all of those things and then be thankful for everything else you have as well. Dig deep. See things with new appreciation. If something in your life is challenging at the moment, see if you can find something in that situation to be thankful for. Think about the things you have that others don't and be thankful for that. Look at small things, big things. Old things, new things. You may find your list is almost infinite.

PRINCIPLE 9 – CHOOSE TO LOVE

It is not a lack of love, but a lack of friendship that makes unhappy marriages.
– Friedrich Nietzsche

Before having kids, there was a time where I was doing really well at work. I was getting selected for special projects and traveling on exciting business trips. I was getting promotions and raises, bigger offices, and more and more responsibility. To keep up, I was going into the office early and leaving late. Often, I would work late into the evening at home as well. I was giving work everything I had and I can confidently say that work was happy to have me around.

You know who wasn't so happy to have me around? My husband. During this time, I was giving work my best self and whenever I did emerge from the office to come home, James was left with an exhausted, irritable person whose mind was still on clients and budgets and deadlines. Any conversation we had during that time would be brought back around to me and my workday. I would fall asleep while James was talking to me, and I was constantly distracted, stressed, unhappy, and generally unpleasant to be around.

Now before you judge me, take a look at yourself and see if you might be guilty of some of this behaviour as well. We have all been there at one time or another. If you had asked me what my number one priority was at that time, I would have said my relationships and family and yet, if you looked at where I was putting my effort, it was work. I think that is partially why I was so unhappy during that time, despite achieving successes at work. Too often our internal ideas of what things are important to us aren't accurately reflected in the distribution of our time and effort.

If you ask any parent what their priorities are, family will usually be number one; however, just as I was doing with work, we give our best selves to the activities that are a lower priority – things like work, errands, and social obligations. Then, whatever energy we have left is generally given to our kids. Our relationships with our husbands or wives get pushed aside, becoming neglected and dusty. Sometimes it gets so bad that we don't even extend to our loved ones the same courtesies we would give to our clients, neighbours, or even strangers. Tell me honestly: are you more likely to hold the door open for your spouse or a client? Unfortunately, this lack of courtesy can extend even to how we talk about our partners. It is not out of the ordinary to hear parents talking about their spouses like they are an incompetent co-worker, not their partners in life.

Children can put a strain on a relationship. Especially in the early days of having kids, we are not at our best. We are tired. So, so tired. We are also dealing with a lot of things that are new to us. We can get moody and we can forget the basic things we should be doing to have a healthy relationship with our spouse.

When life gets busy, it's easy for the time and energy you give your spouse to be the first thing cut from your to-do list. It's important, however, to make a conscious effort to make your husband or wife a priority. Both halves of the couple need to do this, but because we are only in control of ourselves, not our spouses, we need to start with out own attitudes and behaviours. Remember to consider each other and think about ways your time and energy can better match what your overall priorities are. You may not be able to spend the majority of your day on the people who are most important in your life, but you can remember to keep a little bit of your sparkle for them.

If you feel your relationship with your spouse is stronger than ever before, please feel free to skip to the next chapter. If you think you can do better, here are a few places I have chosen to start with my own relationship.

When we love someone our love becomes demonstrable or real only through our exertion – through the fact that for that someone (or for ourself) we take an extra step or walk an extra mile. Love is not effortless. To the contrary, love is effortful.
– M. Scott Peck

First is to choose to love them. So often people assume love is something that just happens. It should just be there and you should have a loving feeling all the time and that will be enough to carry you into being old and grey. For some, that may be true, but there will be times where you simply need to *decide* to love your spouse. To choose to love and let the other things go.

I will give you an example. A few years ago, I got angry at James for not letting me know he would be home late for dinner. It isn't something he usually does. He had been so frantic at work that he had lost track of time. Regardless, I was angry and I decided to take the dog for a walk to get some air. Unfortunately, rather than using the walk to calm down, I was replaying everything in my head and getting myself more worked up. As I was getting more and more mad, I could see our evening together was about to deteriorate. I would come home from my walk angry; I wouldn't want to talk about it, or at least I wouldn't be pacified by talking about it, James would be annoyed and defensive, and we would lose the night to being angry and bitter.

Thankfully, I was snapped out of my thoughts by laughter coming from my neighbours' house. At the time, we lived a few doors down from a busily retired couple in their seventies who were always smiling. I looked over and saw them sitting together on their porch. They were turned away from me and didn't know I was there. She had her hand on his arm and they were talking and laughing together. Not just giggles or polite laughter, but real belly laughter. Just the two of them. I couldn't remember the last time James and I had taken a moment like that to enjoy an evening to simply be in each other's company. It seems we were always too busy. Rushing to do one thing or another, wasting time watching TV instead of spending time talking, running after the kids, or catching up on work.

In that moment, I decided I wanted to choose to love. I didn't want to be angry anymore. I wanted to have a nice evening with my husband who I adore. I wanted to sit together and talk – talk about happy things. I wanted to laugh and I wanted to do that until we were a busily retired couple in our seventies.

It was that easy. My desire to have a nice, happy evening with my husband trumped the relatively insignificant thing I was angry about. It trumped my feeling of wanting to be right or to prove my point. All I had to do was decide to let it go and return to the house with a happy, open attitude; then, rather than having a wasted evening of arguments and bad feelings, we could have a wonderful evening spending time together. That is exactly what happened. I went home happy, that made James happy, and we had a nice evening together. Even better, we have been able to have many more happy evenings together, because my whole perspective shifted that day. If I get angry, I think of my neighbour's belly laughter on that porch and her hand lovingly touching her husband's arm and I know I want that feeling, that happiness, that love, more than I want anything else.

There are so many ways and times happy couples choose to love instead of choosing to fester in unhappiness. Just like everything else, it is a way of thinking and a mindset that can lead you to being happy.

The next thing I try to remember, in my own relationship, is to be nice. We are always telling this to children. Be nice. We need to make sure we aren't just saying this to our kids but are also taking our own advice. I would much rather be nice to someone than be mean. Turns out it isn't just me. Studies have shown that being nice does make people happier.[13]

Being nice takes a little effort and time and nothing else. It doesn't cost anything and it doesn't take anything away from you. It just involves thinking of the other person, considering them and their feelings. Put yourself in their shoes for a minute. What would make them happy? What do they enjoy that they haven't done lately? If something is weighing on them, how can you help make it better?

Being nice to your spouse can be as easy as listening to them with your full attention, making eye contact, or being excited to see them

---

[13] University of Oxford, "Being Kind to Others Does Make You 'Slightly Happier'," *Science Daily*, October 5, 2016, www.sciencedaily.com/releases/2016/10/161005102254.htm (accessed February 13,2018).

when they arrive home. It could also be making them their favourite dinner or picking up a book you think they would like. It might be taking the kids to the park on Sunday morning so they can sleep in or it might be carving out time for them to do something they love like reading, going to a game with friends, or going to the gym. But it also doesn't have to be that complicated.

It can be doing something you know they would appreciate from you. Clean up after yourself. Put your dishes in the dishwasher instead of leaving them in the sink. Leave them a note to tell them where you are or that you love them. Compliment them on the good job they are doing as husband or wife, father or mother. Encourage them when they are down and celebrate with them when they are happy.

A natural concern might be that by doing this, the relationship will become one-sided. You will be putting in all the effort and your spouse will be reaping all the benefit while maintaining their same lack of courtesy toward you. While I wouldn't encourage only being nice to someone so they are nice back to you, I also understand no one wants to be anyone's doormat. My thought is this: it's worth a shot. You have nothing to lose and you have a happily-ever-after to gain. As you start to add in small niceties, I believe you will see your spouse reflecting those niceties back to you. It may not happen immediately, because behaviour patterns can be stubborn to change, but with a little dedication, I firmly believe you will see an improvement in your interactions and relationship.

Adopting this behaviour doesn't have to be an extra task you need to remember to do in addition to all the other things you already have on your mind as a person, spouse, and parent. It doesn't need to be grand in nature and it doesn't need to put you out. It's simply making an effort to be kind, respectful, and loving and as you get into the habit of doing this, you will see it starts to take no effort at all. It simply becomes the new way you interact with each other.

Author Simon Sinek believes it is small niceties that are the reason people fall in love with each other.[14] These are the things that build up over time and tie us together. A single grand gesture won't make someone love someone else; you need to show people daily

[14] Simon Sinek and Tom Bilyeu, "Question Your Motives – Simon Sinek | Inside Quest #74," YouTube video, 100:53, posted by "Tom Bilyeu Classics," May 14, 2017, https://youtu.be/LiKWQQ6J7EI.

that you care through small niceties. Things like making them a tea when you make one for yourself, or asking how their day was and truly caring about the answer.

One person's niceties will be different from another person's. Find the ways you can be nice to your spouse and I guarantee you will be happier for it.

Next, stop bickering. Now, I'm not talking about disagreements – all couples disagree and argue sometimes. I'm talking about bickering, which I see as the result of not working through a disagreement in a grown-up, constructive way. Bickering is one of the most pointless things you can do in a marriage. It doesn't benefit either party, is annoying to both people, and puts everyone – including those around you – in a terrible mood.

True disagreements and issues need to be addressed so that negative feelings can be let go of. A constant, underlying issue will wear on people and set the tone for more and more negativity. Just as we discussed how our children are like mirrors, picking up our moods and reflecting them back to us, we can expect the same with our spouses. How we treat someone is going to reflect how they treat us. It's the reason why, if one person in a couple comes into a room ready for a fight, chances are they will get one.

When things aren't properly resolved, couples start bickering about little things that are of no consequence. A husband might get angry at his wife for being bossy but he is really angry that she is constantly undermining his authority with the kids. A wife might get angry at her husband for leaving dishes in the sink but she really feels unappreciated for the work she is doing around the house. Don't let bad feelings and anger consume you, to be carried around for days and weeks (sometimes years). The person that type of anger hurts most is you.

If you find you are doing a lot of bickering, or receiving a lot of bickering, try to identify the root of the problem and tackle that. Then try to see things from the other person's perspective. Understand that their perception of the situation is their reality. I will say that again because it is important: the other person's perception of the situation *is their reality*. It doesn't matter how *you* think they should see things or feel things; how they see things or feel things is what you need to consider. Examine what you can do to improve things. The only element you are in control of is how you react to a situation. You can't control others or their reactions and you can't make people do or think the things you want them to. That is true of your spouse, your kids, your parents, and everyone else you know now or will ever come in contact with. If you want to be happy, you need to start with yourself. Remember, no one can make you behave in a certain way or think something you don't want to think or even feel something you don't want to feel. You alone control your behaviour, thoughts, and feelings. Use them in constructive ways.

Next, have sex. Remember when you were young and you realized your parents had sex and thought it was super gross? You were wrong. Kids want their parents to have sex. They want their parents to have sex because it is part of a healthy and happy relationship and if their parents are not having sex, they are missing out on a lot of emotional and health benefits, not to mention the actual fun of having sex.

Personally, I'm not one to talk about sex. I was raised like most girls are. Nice girls don't talk about sex and they don't have sex. Once you are married, the rule book says it is OK to have sex but no one comes over and says, "Hey, good work on keeping all the sex stuff on the down low for all these years. Now you can feel totally comfortable and be open with it." Having spent a lifetime with it being taboo, many people tend not to chat about it much. In fact, I was so uncomfortable discussing sex with my parents that I was nervous to tell them I was pregnant because then they would definitively know I had sex. I was 32 years old and married but judging by how sweaty my palms were, you would have thought I was a teenager who had just been caught with a boy in my room.

The reason I am bringing it up in this book is because sex is really, really important. While it can be somewhat awkward to talk about, it is worse not to. Especially when there is a problem. Having a problem you feel you can't talk about can be an isolating, sad, and lonely experience.

It is a misperception that it is "just sex." Touch, intimacy, and sex are so important both to a relationship and to a person's health and happiness. Sex has been shown to improve immunity, improve heart health, lower blood pressure, relieve pain, lower the risk of prostate cancer, relieve stress, improve sleep and improve bladder control (here's looking at you, postpartum moms). In addition, it will help you feel more bonded to your partner, and having sex will make you want to have more sex.[15] Did I mention it also counts as exercise? I mean, if there were a miracle drug, it would appear sex is it.

Oddly enough, a side effect of having kids – the result of sex – is often a lack of touch and intimacy, and that can have a devastating effect on a marriage. Fatigue, stress, and "headaches" are all culprits. I get it. Sometimes you just want one moment in your day where someone isn't sticking their hands up or down your shirt, pulling your hair, or sitting on your face. You just want one moment when you are not being touched. Kids take a boatload of our time, attention, and energy but we still need to remember to make ourselves and our relationship with our spouse a priority, too.

Many people just don't feel like sex after having kids. There is a period of recovery and exhaustion after having a baby when sex simply won't be in the cards. To say that is completely understandable is an understatement. But after a period of time, sex is put back on the table and this is when tensions can start to rise. If both halves of the couple feel like sex, there is no issue. Congratulations and go to town. If both halves of the couple don't feel like sex, there is no issue. Some may argue they are missing out on the health benefits of the miracle drug but at least no one's feelings are getting hurt. The real issue is when only one half of the couple doesn't want to have sex, leaving the other half feeling hurt, rejected, and disconnected. When there is an imbalance in sexual desire, it is a short trip to the place where arguments and discomfort will start to surround sex and the topic of sex. Other forms of affection start to fade and suddenly you have an angry, cold roommate, not a loving, warm spouse.

Michele Weiner-Davis is a relationship expert with a TED Talk called The Sex Starved Marriage and she has figured out a simple solution to the problem.[16] The solution is to have sex. Weiner-Davis

---

[15] Dr. Mercola, "Study: How Often Do Happy People Have Sex?" *Mercola*, April 28, 2016, https://articles.mercola.com/sites/articles/archive/2016/04/28/healthy-sex-life-benefits.aspx (accessed February 13, 2018)

[16] Michele Weiner-Davis, "The Sex-Starved Marriage | Michele Weiner-Davis | TEDxCU," YouTube video, 17:35, posted by "TEDx Talks," April 29,2014, https://youtu.be/Ep2MAx95m20.

believes in order to have a healthy relationship the people in that relationship sometimes need to put the other person's needs above their own. The person with the lower sex drive needs to remember sex is fun and to just do it. Once they get into it, they remember they like it and things improve. The couple is happier, there is less strain. It is also important to mention that Weiner-Davis says low sex drive isn't a female issue, as many people assume; men experience low sex drive as well, and women feel the rejection and hurt that comes along with that just as strongly, if not more so, since the assumption is that men want sex all the time.

Being able to touch, hug, kiss, and have sex with your spouse whenever you want is a wonderful perk of marriage. It is inexpensive, good for you, and fun. Take advantage.

My last piece of marriage advice comes from an article I once read with advice from successful couples. One couple, Anne and Joseph Gaston had been married for over 60 years. Anne Gaston's marriage advice was "don't be afraid to be the person who loves the most."[17] That advice has resonated with me on many occasions. We are always taught to try to get the upper hand, to have the advantage, and to be the one on top. That might be relevant when you first start dating someone and you don't want to be their doormat but once you are with someone who loves you and who you trust, you shouldn't be burdened with power struggles. You are free to love unconditionally and completely because, if you are in the right kind of relationship, both people in the couple are thinking of one another. You should be your spouse's cheering squad, support system, shoulder to cry on, person to lean on. You should make them a better person and conversely, you should feel as though you are a better person because of them.

I love Gaston's advice. It reminds me not to hold a grudge or insist on being right. It tells me to give my husband the time and freedom to pursue his interests and dreams. It urges me to apologize when I am wrong, and to be patient when he is not. I want him to feel supported always because I know how much his support has helped me and how much it continues to help me. What a wonderful

---

[17] Nate Bagley, "Don't Be Afraid To Be The One Who Loves The Most," *The Loveumentary*, July 24, 2014, https://loveumentary.com/blog/dont-be-afraid-to-be-the-one-who-loves-the-most (accessed on February 13, 2018)

gift to be able to give someone.

As a final thought in this chapter, I want to mention that having a healthy relationship with our spouses doesn't only benefit us. It benefits our kids too. We learn how to behave in relationships by watching our parents. We learn how to deal with conflict, relate to each other, be affectionate, have constructive conversations, share interests, show support. Make sure the example you are setting is a positive one that sets them up for happy relationships in their future as well.

The best security blanket a child can have is parents who respect each other.
– Jane Blaustone

HOMEWORK

Do something nice for your spouse.

PRINCIPLE 10 - BE NICE TO YOURSELF

Almost anything will work again if you unplug it for a few minutes, including you
– Anne Lamott

You know how flight attendants always tell parents to put the oxygen masks on themselves before assisting young children? At first glance, it seems stupid. What adult is going to leave a child without life-giving oxygen while they help themselves to their own delicious oxygen? It seems selfish and it just doesn't feel right to help ourselves before our kids. But then, of course, you realize that if the adults don't help themselves first, they could wind up in a situation where they cannot help either the child or themselves.

The same thinking can be applied in everyday life with children. Parents are often so focused on the kids and on doing everything perfectly, they forget to take care of themselves. As someone smarter than me once said, "You are not required to set yourself on fire to keep others warm."

But we are all guilty of setting ourselves on fire from time to time. Sometimes more often than that. A few years ago, I sent out a Christmas card that had a family photo on it. A few days later, I got a text from one of my oldest friends, who wrote: "Thanks for the card but what's with the photo?"

I was confused. What does he mean, what's with the photo? So I texted him back, "What do you mean, what's with the photo?"

"You look awful," he replied.

EXCUSE me? Awful? If I hadn't known him since we were 12, I would have never spoken to him again. As it was, I was definitely not speaking with him until the New Year. Awful? What does he know? I don't look awful. Where is that stupid card anyway?

When I found the card, I had to admit he was not wrong. I mean, his delivery could use some work, but he wasn't wrong. Like most parents, I hadn't been focusing on myself. I was completely consumed with the kids. I hadn't gotten a full night's sleep in months, I wasn't exercising or eating well. On the day the photo was taken, I was so focused on getting the kids ready that I ran out of time to do my own makeup or blow dry my hair. Looking back, it's a wonder I was even wearing clothes that day, because making sure the kids (who were zero and two at the time) didn't get dirty before the picture took 200 per cent of my attention.

There are always a million reasons why parents put themselves last. *I can't read that book I got because I should be paying attention to the kids. I shouldn't spend money on clothes for myself because the baby really needs a 12th patterned muslin blanket. It's selfish of me to take my neighbour up on her offer to watch the baby while I go have a coffee and do the crossword. Who needs showers when dry shampoo exists?* Parents are forever finding reasons to put the needs of others above their own and as I stared at the under-eye bags on my Christmas card, I could see the error of my ways. Unfortunately, so could all my closest friends and family because all the cards had already been mailed out.

Although it is hard to give ourselves any attention when we are caring for our kids, it is really important to try to take good care of yourself as well. Do not feel guilty about taking time for yourself. It will benefit you and it will benefit your kids. Setting ourselves on fire is not healthy or sustainable. Let's talk about some of the basic things parents need for themselves in order to be properly functioning, and healthy.

We all need water and food to survive. Make sure you are drinking plenty of water and eating food that will give you energy and not just satisfy cravings or hunger in the moment. Finding a free moment (or hand) to prepare food can be a challenge for parents, especially new parents, but try to keep healthy foods in the house and plan ahead whenever possible. Without proper nutrition, you will get even more run down, your energy will drop, you won't think as well, and you'll get irritable. Eating properly and staying hydrated will help you to be at your best.

Sleep. We all need sleep. Not an easy thing to come by with kids, but again, we need to try our best to get as much rest as possible. If you aren't getting enough sleep at night, make sure you make sleep a priority in the day as well. If you get a free moment – someone else comes to help or your baby is napping – leave any other things you have to do and get some sleep yourself. The dishes, laundry, and reading this book can wait. Trust me.

Another thing we are meant to do as human beings is go outside. Studies show that when we engage with nature, we have increased happiness and health.[18] Unfortunately, many new parents don't get outside as much as they should, and that can be bad for our moods and mental health. Young kids now spend considerably less time outdoors than previous generations have.[19] It's important to re-establish our connection to nature. Find a hiking trail, beach or local park, and spend some time there as part of your regular routine. It will be beneficial for everyone.

Exercise. Don't look at me like that. You knew it was coming. There is just no way around it. Exercise is incredibly beneficial to both our physical and mental health. Exercise will make you happier and more relaxed, give you more energy to tackle the day, reduce health risks, improve the quality of your sleep, make you stronger and more confident, and even boost your sex life.[20] The benefits are endless. Of course, when kids are small it may not be the time in your life when you can spend endless hours in a gym, nor will it be the time when you will be in the best shape of your life, but try to get *some* exercise. As a parent, there are plenty of ways to get exercise. These days there are lots of baby and me classes, you can use a

---

[18] Richardson, M., Cormack, A., McRobert, L. & Underhill, R., "30 Days Wild: Development and Evaluation of a Large-Scale Nature Campaign to Improve Well-Being," *PLoS ONE*, February 18, 2016, 11(2): e0149777. doi:10.1371/journal.pone.0149777

[19] Clements, R., "An Investigation of the Status of Outdoor Play," *Contemporary Issues in Early Childhood*, Vol.5, No. 1, March 2004, 68-80.

[20] "You Know Exercise is Good For You, But Do You Know How Good? From Boosting Your Mood to Improving Your Sex Life, Find Out How Exercise Can Improve Your Life," *Mayo Clinic*, October 13, 2016, http://www.mayoclinic.org/healthy-lifestyle/fitness/in-depth/exercise/art-20048389 (accessed February 14, 2018).

jogging stroller to jog or bike ride with the kids, you can join a gym that has a childcare area for parents or, if all that seems like too much work or too expensive, you can always workout at home with online videos. If there is no time for a video, take a few minutes to run your stairs or do some squats while you hold the baby or brush your teeth. Even 60 seconds will do you some good.

There you have it. People need healthy food and water, sleep, fresh air, and exercise. All people need that. Even supermom and superdad.

The next part of being nice to yourself is probably the harder one for parents today. The next thing you need to do is give yourself a break.

There are no perfect parents. Just as there are no perfect children..
– Fred Rogers

People are so hard on themselves these days. Parents put pressure on themselves to be perfect and they expect perfection from day one. They set unrealistic expectations for themselves based on what they see in movies or read in books. They are told a parent should know how to identify their baby's different cries, that they should be able to soothe their children on demand, and that their babies should sleep soundly through the night. Images of celebrity parents with their new babies, all perfectly styled, are in every check-out line, and we feel we should look just as wonderful a week into having a new baby. Social media also plays on our minds as we compare ourselves to our peers and judge ourselves harshly, even though we only see highly-curated snapshots of what other people's lives are actually like.

In reality, all parents are going to struggle. Someone once told me it takes six months to get used to a new job. Not necessarily the work, but all the little things that crop up in the day – how to fix the paper jam in the photocopier, where meeting room 9A is, and where all the files are on the shared drives. It is the same when you are a new parent. You know the basics of the job. You need to feed the baby and change their diapers, but why are they crying, why won't they sleep, and how do you wash these slippery little suckers? What's even more challenging is that this new job involves taking care of the most precious thing in the world to you; on top of that, you are compromised because you are sleep-deprived, in totally new circumstances, and there is no one available for onboarding training. As soon as you think you have the hang of it, the job changes again. They start walking, talking and then talking back. Your skill set needs to be continually adapting to a moving target.

As parents, we need to keep things in perspective and be kind to ourselves. The first years of having kids is a trying time. There are crying spells and temper tantrums, potty training pressures and added expenses. In the moment, it can seem like these times will never end. Remember to take a step back and realize that these things are all part of a larger story. They are all temporary.

Sometimes, when we are very focused on our day-to-day, it is hard to remember that everything we are doing is part of a bigger picture. If you aren't your best self one day, if you experience a set back, don't beat yourself up. We all suck at it sometimes. It is just a moment, a day, even a year in a whole lifetime. We are working on an impressionist painting. Don't worry if your individual brushstrokes are a mess. They will all come together to reveal something great once you step back and appreciate it as a whole.

By taking the time to look at the big picture, we gain invaluable perspective on what is important. Not just important today, but important to us overall. We get bogged down in dishes and diapers and paying bills and running errands. That stuff can wait. Where do we want to spend our time and resources? Focus on the big things. It might mean the dishes need to stay in the sink for a few hours while we go for a walk or enjoy some finger painting but that's OK. You will remember the finger painting but you won't remember the dishes.

Be easy on yourself. Not just because you deserve it but so you have the energy and courage to go at it again the next day. No one is perfect. When you make mistakes or don't get it all done, don't beat yourself up. Just try again tomorrow.

RECAP

1. Decide to be Happy
2. Avoid Negativity
3. Think for Yourself
4. Have a Goal
5. Do One Thing at a Time
6. Accept What You Can't Control
7. Give Your Full Effort
8. Appreciate What You Have
9. Choose to Love
10. Be Nice to Yourself

ACKNOWLEDGMENTS

Thank you to Jane Warren for teaching me to only put one space after a period (amongst other things).

Thank you to all my friends and family for being the people I can always depend on for support and encouragement. Knowing such smart and wonderful people believe in me, makes me believe in myself.

Finally, thank you to my husband for always being the person who I knew I married; and to my kids, Sharkey and Jack, for filling me up with more joy than I could have ever imagined.

ABOUT THE AUTHOR

Linsey Nogueira Flannery is a public relations executive turned stay-at-home mom. She lives in Toronto, Canada with her husband and two children. *Unfudge Yourself: A Parent's Guide to Happiness* is her first book.

Made in the USA
Columbia, SC
27 December 2020

29868832R00067